The
Ready
or
Knot
Prayer Guide

The
Ready
or
Knot

Prayer Guide

100 Prayers for Dating and Engaged Couples

SCOTT KEDERSHA

BakerBooks

a division of Baker Publishing Group
Grand Rapids, Michigan

Published by Baker Books
a division of Baker Publishing Group
Grand Rapids, Michigan
www.bakerbooks.com

Printed in the United States of America

Library of Congress Cataloging-in-Publication Data
Names: Kedersha, Scott, 1973– author.
Title: The ready or knot prayer guide : 100 prayers for dating and engaged couples
    / Scott Kedersha.
Description: Grand Rapids, Michigan : Baker Books, a division of Baker
    Publishing Group, [2023] | Includes bibliographical references.
Identifiers: LCCN 2022051805 | ISBN 9781540902870 (cloth) | ISBN
    9781493443284 (ebook)
Subjects: LCSH: Married people—Prayers and devotions. | Married people—
    Religious life. | Marriage—Religious aspects—Christianity.
Classification: LCC BV4596.M3 K43 2023 | DDC 248.8/44—dc23/eng/20230130
LC record available at https://lccn.loc.gov/2022051805

Unless otherwise indicated, Scripture quotations are from THE HOLY
BIBLE, NEW INTERNATIONAL
VERSION®, NIV® Copyright © 1973,
1978, 1984, 2011 by Biblica, Inc.®
Used by permission. All rights reserved
worldwide.

Scripture quotations marked ESV are
from The Holy Bible, English Standard
Version® (ESV®), copyright © 2001
by Crossway, a publishing ministry of
Good News Publishers. Used by permission. All rights reserved. ESV Text
Edition: 2016.

Italics added to Scripture quotations are
the author's emphasis.

Some personal names and identifying
details have been changed to protect
the privacy of the individuals involved.

The information in this book is intended
for educational purposes only and
should not substitute for professional
medical, psychological, or legal advice.
Especially in cases of abuse or addiction,
always consult a professional.

Baker Publishing Group publications
use paper produced from sustainable
forestry practices and post-consumer
waste whenever possible.

23 24 25 26 27 28 29   7 6 5 4 3 2 1

This book is dedicated to two couples I greatly admire:

To Jim and Judy Wimberley—
Thank you for modeling a prayer-filled life.
None of us will ever know this side
of heaven the impact of your decades
of prayers for so many people.
Eternities have changed, marriages
have been healed, and joy has been found.
Jim, thanks for being my best friend.

To Byron and Carla Weathersbee—
You've been doing marriage ministry for longer
than most readers of this book have been alive!
You and the ministry you lead have deeply impacted
the marriages of many of my greatest friends.
Thank you for pouring into their marriages
and for doing the same for Kristen and me.

May every couple who reads this book
follow in your footsteps as you follow Christ.

Contents

Communication and Conflict

Spiritual Intimacy

Understanding Your Spouse

Money

Roles

Emotional Intimacy

Sexual Intimacy

Parents and In-Laws

Contents

Foreword

The Lord made it very clear I was to go into vocational ministry. Then, as He often does when He makes something clear, He showed me where I was to work. The church my wife and I attended called and offered me a job. There were a few challenges with this plan. I'd never considered working for a church, so I had zero formal ministry training. We were newly married, and my sweet wife had entered into a covenant with someone in business development committed to worldly success, not a minister. She was willing to go wherever the Lord took us, but working at a church would mean some major lifestyle adjustments. We'd have to sell our new house, eat out much less, and consider many shifts to adhere to a new budget.

I'd been walking with the Lord for less than five years. What did I know about ministry? It felt like I was closing my eyes and jumping off a cliff into the unknown. I had so many questions. And it wasn't only that I *felt* unqualified; I was, in fact, very unqualified. How would I learn to do ministry? My first day came, and I moved from my high-rise office in the city to Watermark Community Church, in Dallas. The church was rapidly growing and adding to their staff. I had somehow snuck in, but they didn't really have a place to put me. There was a closet on the seventh floor. That's not a metaphor—it was an interior closet with no windows. It was a large closet, and I learned I'd share it with someone else who was starting on staff about the same time. That was when I met Scott Kedersha.

Scott was a kind, down-to-earth man, raised on the East Coast. His shoulders bounced when he laughed, and he asked open-ended questions with a deep sincerity. Those are the two expressions he would alternate between: sincerity and laughter. His journey to ministry couldn't have been more different from mine. He interned at a large church, graduated from a well-known seminary, and knew that he wanted to work for a church. His background, however, was like mine. Before getting serious about his faith, he drank deeply from the world. There we were, two new pastors, each having our own desk but sharing a closet. We affectionately called it the cloffice.

Scott would become my go-to source for answers, and I had a lot of questions. "Who wrote Genesis?" "How do we reconcile predestination and free will?" "Is cussing a sin?" These are not questions pastors should ask, but Scott was not afraid of them. He was patient with me. We got to know each other quickly, sharing such a small space five days a week. Scott became one of the greatest pastors I have ever known.

The thing that stood out most to me about Scott was his marriage to Kristen. My wife, Monica, and I had lots of problems in communication and conflict resolution. Scott's marriage seemed almost too good to be true. As I got to know him better, I learned how hard they worked for that reality. It wasn't too good to be true. It was a reality, but it was hard fought for. They loved each other and their family. I admired this most about Scott.

Fast-forward seventeen years, and it's not surprising that Scott has become one of the most renowned marriage pastors on the planet. As for me, Scott's answers laid a foundation for me to pastor a church. When I was looking for someone to help me with marriages, you better believe I called Scott. He moved his family to partner with us here in Waco, Texas. His writing on marriage has helped people around the world. He, along with the research of many others, has discovered that prayer is key to a successful marriage. In the pages ahead, Scott is going to guide you toward praying for the marriage you've always dreamed of. Whether you're ready or (k)not.

Jonathan "JP" Pokluda, lead pastor of Harris Creek Baptist Church; author of *Why Do I Do What I Don't Want to Do?* and *Outdated*

Introduction

What I Wish I Knew before I Said "I Do"

The two questions I'm most often asked as a marriage pastor are, "What's something you're glad you did from day one of marriage?" and "What's the one thing you wish you'd started from day one of marriage?" There are a bunch of answers to the first question, including the fact that I'm grateful that as newlyweds, Kristen and I walked through life with other couples in our church's small group community, we served together in our church, and we each read our Bibles daily. But there's only one answer to the second question: I wish Kristen and I had prayed together every day, even before we said "I do."

Too many Christian marriages end up like the marriages of the world. Between high divorce rates and couples who seem bored and stuck, it's easy to look around and wonder if it's possible to be happily married. During my almost two decades of full-time marriage ministry, I've sat with many struggling or divorced couples who wished they'd handled their marriages differently. The good news is that I've also worked with thousands of couples who have thriving, healthy marriages. I've seen over and over that the habit of praying together daily can draw spouses closer together and help them become more like Jesus Christ.

The couple who prays together stays together. It might be cliché, but it's true. A recent study showed the divorce rate for couples who pray together on a consistent basis is less than 1 percent.[1] Can you believe that? Less than 1 percent of couples who pray together consistently end up divorced. While praying together does not guarantee a perfect, joyful marriage, it certainly provides some protection against the painful consequences of divorce. Not only that, but praying together will also grow your relationship with each other and, even more importantly, with the Lord. I've seen many couples establish a healthy and consistent prayer life from day one of marriage.

I wrote my first book, *Ready or Knot? 12 Conversations Every Couple Needs to Have before Marriage*, because I wanted couples to have an authentic, biblical, practical guide to help discern the best next step in their relationship and to strengthen their future marriage.[2] *The Ready or Knot Prayer Guide* picks up where my first book left off by providing one hundred daily devotions to guide you and your future spouse in having these conversations with the Lord through prayer.

This book is designed to help you begin praying daily for your future marriage. It might even lead some of you to realize you or your significant other aren't ready for marriage together—and trust me, that's a good thing to know *before* you say "I do."

Green Light, Yellow Light, or Red Light?

In *Ready or Knot?* I discussed the comparison between a traffic light and a dating or engaged relationship. When we're driving, a green light tells us to keep moving forward, a yellow light warns us to slow down, and a red light tells us to stop. In the same way, a green light in your relationship tells you to move forward toward engagement or marriage. A yellow light tells you that you need to slow down and figure out next steps. A red light tells you that you should end the relationship.

As you work through this prayer guide with your significant other, I want you to keep this stoplight analogy in mind. While you read about and pray through the Christlike traits needed for a successful marriage, evaluate how you're doing in your relationship. Does each of you possess the attributes discussed in this book? Does your significant other desire to grow in these characteristics to become more like Jesus Christ? If outsiders looked at your relationship, would they see you model these traits together?

I've heard it said that the best predictor of future behavior is current behavior. In other words, if you want to be humble in the future, then examine your life and ask yourself if you're humble today. If you want to be resilient in your marriage, then ask yourself if you're resilient in your life right now. This book is not about your hopeful aspirations but about current reality in your life, your significant other's life, and your relationship.

I'm hopeful that as you pray through these devotions together, the Lord would make it clear to you if you have a green, yellow, or red light in your relationship. While red lights are painful and scary, they can prevent you from entering a marriage you want no part of. A yellow light alerts you to areas you need to discuss and prayerfully consider. And a green light will hopefully help you move forward to the next stage of your relationship.

I want your wedding day to be filled with joy and excitement. Marriage is scary enough for most couples, but it becomes flat-out terrifying if you choose to marry the wrong person. Use the next one hundred days of going through this prayer guide to help you determine next steps.

The Purpose of This Prayer Guide

A few years ago, a friend reached out to me via email and asked, "Scott, I'm getting married in seven days, and I'd like to be intentional in how I use my time and prayers the next week. What are some specific character traits and Scriptures I could pray over the next week (my last as a single man!) that would help strengthen me to be a loving, caring, and godly husband?"

I was encouraged by my friend's email and responded to him with several traits and Scriptures.[3] When I hit send, I immediately knew this could be a great resource for premarried couples. His question helped lead to the origin of this prayer guide, which encourages seriously dating couples and engaged men and women to pray together as they prepare to say "I do."

The *Ready or Knot Prayer Guide* covers ninety-six attributes you will pray for yourself, for your significant other, and for your marriage. These traits revolve around the twelve conversations in the *Ready or Knot?* book. Each devotion features a daily Bible verse, as well as other verses throughout the discussion. I've started with four entries that will help you discern how to pray together as a seriously dating or an engaged couple. These one hundred devotions are designed to help you establish a pattern of praying together that will propel you into a prayer-dependent, Christ-centered marriage.

The traits you'll pray through in this prayer guide are the ones that stick out in a Christian marriage. These are not some random traits that may or may not help a marriage. These are characteristics that, when possessed by both husband and wife, lead to thriving, attractive marriages. I encourage you to pray through each of these essential traits. My hope is that you and your significant other will live out these Christlike attributes in your lives and future marriage. No one can do so perfectly, but you can ask God to help you grow these traits more and more in your lives.

The goal of this guide is not primarily that you would have a great marriage. That might seem like a strange statement. *Why doesn't the marriage guy want us to have a great marriage?* I do, but that's not the primary goal. The main purpose of this prayer guide is to help each of you become more like Jesus Christ. I believe the key to a healthy Christian marriage is for a man who wholeheartedly loves Jesus to marry a woman who wholeheartedly loves Jesus.

I hope and pray this resource will strengthen your relationship as you seek the Lord together. I pray it will tune your heart to His and help you establish a pattern of prayer you will follow for the rest of your days as husband and wife. And I pray you will seek the Lord together as a couple all the days He gives you breath.

Ready or knot? Let's pray.

DAY 1

Are We Allowed to Pray Together before Marriage?

So, if you think you are standing firm, be careful that you don't fall! No temptation has overtaken you except what is common to mankind. And God is faithful; he will not let you be tempted beyond what you can bear. But when you are tempted, he will also provide a way out so that you can endure it.

1 Corinthians 10:12–13

Can you pray together before marriage? Of course you can. Unless someone shows me a Bible passage that says otherwise, I strongly encourage you to pray together before you say "I do." That's the whole point of this prayer guide, that you would take the time to start the habit of praying together before you get married.

When you and your significant other pray together, you gain great insight into each other. You learn more about how you each are growing and where you're each struggling. You get to see each other come before the Lord and pour out your heart to Him. You can learn a lot about someone's spiritual maturity by the way they pray. So, yes, please do pray together before you get married.

But I want to offer a few warnings and encouragements about praying together as a premarried couple:

- *Don't put yourself in a position where you can be tempted to fall into sexual sin.* Praying together is an intimate act. Be careful of where and when you pray. In other words, don't pray in a quiet apartment with no one around, snuggled up on the couch together. The intimacy of prayer can lead you to cross boundaries physically with each other.

- *Determine your motive in praying.* Why are you praying together? Is it to come to the God of the universe and communicate with Him? Is it to pray for your relationship and future marriage? Or are you putting on a show to impress your significant other? Check your motive before you pray together.

- *Don't attempt to manipulate each other through your prayers.* For example, "Lord, please help my partner not to be selfish all the time" is not a prayer I recommend praying. Rather, change the way you pray: "Lord, will You please help us not to be selfish? We're both tempted at times to put our own needs first, but we want to serve and celebrate each other. Please help us, Lord."

Ready? Let's give it a shot!

Lord, please help us to pray together with the right motives and with the right heart posture. Help us to work on ourselves first, and help us not to manipulate each other. Please protect our purity, and help us to honor each other and honor You when we pray together. Thank You that You see us, hear us, and love us.

DAY 2

Why Should My Significant Other and I Pray Together?

You do not have because you do not ask God. When you ask,
you do not receive, because you ask with wrong motives, that
you may spend what you get on your pleasures.

James 4:2–3

Prayer gives us the opportunity to commune with the Lord and
with our significant other. A heart aligned with God's seeks
what He wants and desires for us. The problem is, almost everything we do in life is tainted with selfish motives. In James
4:1, James said we fight and quarrel because of selfish desires
that wage war within us. We argue, complain, and whine when
there's something we want and we don't have it. In verse 3,
James said even our prayers are tainted by our selfish motives.

We can't even pray to the Lord without seeking our pleasures and desires.

Therefore, we need to figure out how to align our prayers with what would most honor the Lord. Praying together with your significant other gives you the opportunity to seek the Lord's best for your lives and for His own glory.

There's not much on this planet that will strengthen a relationship and draw a couple closer to the Lord and each other more than prayer. Prayer builds resilient marriages, grows intimacy between a husband and wife, and draws each spouse closer to Christ. The couple who prays together recognizes the greatness of God and His lordship over their lives. When you and your significant other pray for specific Christlike attributes, you acknowledge you fall short but are aware He desires to help you grow.

We all go through ups and downs, and prayer is inconsistent at best for most couples. To build the habit of daily prayer into your lives from day one of your life together, I strongly encourage you and your significant other to start praying for your marriage before you say "I do!"

Lord, sometimes we don't know how or why to pray. But we want to. We want to honor You, and we want our prayers to honor You, not to win Your favor but so that we can grow in intimacy with You. We realize we often pray with selfish motives, so help us align our prayers with Your desires. Thank You that You hear us and see us, and You always know what we need before a word is even on our lips or hearts.

DAY 3

How Should We Pray Together?

And when you pray, do not be like the hypocrites, for they love to pray standing in the synagogues and on the street corners to be seen by others. Truly I tell you, they have received their reward in full. But when you pray, go into your room, close the door and pray to your Father, who is unseen.

Matthew 6:5–6

If you're like most Christians, you're used to praying by yourself, all alone. It's also possible that you've prayed with groups, such as your community group or Bible study group. But you may not have prayed very often with just one other person, especially someone of the opposite sex. Praying with another person can be awkward or even clunky, so how should you and your significant other pray together?

Here are a few suggestions:

- *Don't try to use big, overly religious words.* Talk to the Lord as you would with any other person. He already knows what you're thinking and every word about to come out of your mouth, so keep it real.

- *Keep it short.* There are times when you and your significant other will pray for longer periods of time, but most of the time you can keep it brief. Ping-pong back and forth as you pray.

- *Pray about anything.* Remember, you're speaking to the God of the universe! Nothing is too big for Him to handle, and nothing is too small to pray about.

- *Don't try to impress each other.* As Jesus said in Matthew 6:5–6, don't pray to be seen and praised. You don't have to literally go into your room, close the door, and pray. But make sure you're not praying to receive the praise of your significant other instead of to connect with the Lord.

- *Add some variety to your prayer posture.* At times you may pray standing with your arms raised. Other times you may find yourself flat on your stomach. However you sit or stand doesn't matter near as much as the posture of your heart. (But keep in mind the caution I mentioned on day 1 to avoid praying together in positions that might tempt you to sin sexually.)

- *Pray the Scriptures.* Sometimes we don't know *what* to pray. I'd suggest praying Scripture back to the Lord. The Psalms, in addition to this prayer guide, are a great place to start doing so.

As you pray with your significant other, ask God to direct your conversations with Him and to guide your words.

Lord, help us not to be awkward with each other as we pray together as a couple. This is new to us, and we don't want to pray to impress each other or try to impress You. We just want to be faithful to seek You and become more like You. Help make praying together a daily practice and discipline for us as a couple. We want to honor You in every way.

DAY 4

What Happens When We Pray?

This is the confidence we have in approaching God: that if we ask anything according to his will, he hears us. And if we know that he hears us—whatever we ask—we know that we have what we asked of him.

1 John 5:14–15

What happens when we pray? The short answer is that I don't know. It blows my mind how the Lord can handle listening to billions of prayers at the same time. His ability to listen to and know everything proves that He is both omniscient (all-knowing) and omnipotent (all-powerful). It's hard enough for me to listen to one person at a time, let alone billions!

Some people think God works like a vending machine—you put money in, and you know exactly what will come out. Put in four quarters for some Reese's Peanut Butter Cups, push the button, and out comes your delicious combination of chocolate and peanut butter. Push the Kit Kat button, and out comes a Kit Kat.

But God doesn't work that way. If He did, when we ask for something like millions of dollars, it would show up in our bank accounts. We'd no longer struggle with sin, and the world would be filled with peace. Part of the problem is that we don't make requests that align with the heart of God; rather, our prayer requests are marked by our own selfish desires.

One of the hopes in prayer is that our desires would align with His. John captured this concept well in 1 John 5:14: "If we ask anything according to his will, he hears us." John encouraged us to pray with God's will in mind, not our own. And therein lies the problem, since our requests tend to be self-centered.

In marriage, part of the reason you pray together is to align your hearts as husband and wife. In the process, your desires begin to align with God's. When you ask Him together for the desires of your hearts, your hearts will hopefully become increasingly aligned with His. Then you know that He will hear you and that you and your future spouse will have whatever you ask of Him—when you ask according to His will.

God, we need Your help as we pray. We know that our prayer requests often reflect our selfish desires. We know You hear every one of our prayers, but it's our desire that our prayers become increasingly aligned with Your heart. We need You, and we need Your help. May we always be dependent upon You.

The Purpose
of Marriage

DAY 5

Holy

As obedient children, do not conform to the evil desires you had when you lived in ignorance. But just as he who called you is holy, so be holy in all you do; for it is written: "Be holy, because I am holy."

1 Peter 1:14–16

The goal of this book is not just to give you tips and tricks for a better marriage. My deepest hope is that you would become more like Jesus Christ. Over and over in the Bible we read that the Lord is holy. And since we're to be like Him, as Peter said, we are to be holy as He is holy.

We're not capable of being perfectly holy and blameless like Jesus. He's the only perfect human in the history of the world. You and I can't go even a few moments without sinning in thought or deed, but we're still called to pursue holiness. That means, as we're faced with thousands of decisions every day, we should aim to choose what honors the Lord.

Gary Thomas, in his excellent marriage book *Sacred Marriage*, asks a profound question: "What if God designed marriage to make us holy more than to make us happy?"[1] While many people get married because they think it will make them happy, the greater goal of marriage is holiness and becoming more like Jesus Christ. There's nothing wrong with the desire to be happy; it's just not the greatest, ultimate desire. In *Ready or Knot?*, I said, "When you marry someone, God intends for you to grow in holiness and to become more like Christ."[2]

There's something deeply profound that happens in healthy marriages. When you pursue Jesus together, you see areas in which you don't reflect Christ. Marriage helps expose areas of struggle and weakness and shines a spotlight on ways you can grow in holiness and become more like Christ. This is a beautiful part of Christian marriage that we don't often discuss. God gives us a spouse to help us become more holy and more like His Son, Jesus.

I believe every attribute in this book is essential for you to have a God-honoring, thriving marriage. Some rise toward the top in importance—this is one of them. Today, ask God to help make you *holy* as He is holy.

> *Lord, thank You that You are perfect and holy. Thank You that You are without spot or blemish. And thank You that You clearly state that You desire holiness for us as well. Help us become more like Your Son, Jesus, and help us to be holy in our marriage. May we make decisions that always drive us to become more like You in every way.*

DAY 6

Steadfast

You will keep in perfect peace those whose minds are steadfast,
because they trust in you.

Isaiah 26:3

In your marriage vows, you and your significant other will
make some big promises: to stay together in sickness, poverty,
and hard times. You will commit to being steadfast—firm and
unwavering—to your spouse. God loves us with a steadfast love,
and your marriage will require the same of you. The way to
experience peace and joy in your marriage is through a steadfast
love and trust in the Lord and in your spouse.

It might seem odd for a premarried couple to pray for steadfastness, but this attribute is central to all healthy marriages.
I've seen the importance of this trait lived out with a friend who
lost her husband of fifty-one years. For twelve years she walked

alongside him through a major stroke and related complications. She stood by his side until he passed away from cancer.

I've seen this kind of steadfastness much closer to home as I watched my mom love and serve my stepdad through his battle with Alzheimer's. For years she cared for him all day, every day, as he battled with the cognitive and physical challenges associated with his disease.

On the premarried side, you have no idea what lies ahead. You can't predict whether you'll experience financial challenges, infertility, wayward children, or struggles with addictions. All any of us know is that in this world we will have troubles (John 16:33).

As you get ready to say "I do," pray that you will be a steadfast spouse: firm, unwavering, and immovable in both the celebrations and trials of life. You won't allow the wins of life to pull you off course in following Jesus, and you won't allow life's challenges to cause you to question the goodness of God. A steadfast spouse remains faithful and unwavering in their trust in the Lord regardless of their circumstances.

During my last seventeen years in full-time marriage ministry, I've watched steadfast couples weather many storms while couples who lacked this trait crumbled under the challenges and pressures of the world. As I type these words, I'm praying that your lives and your future marriage will be marked by steadfastness.

God, help us to be immovable and unwavering in both the victories and challenges of life. Help us to fight together as a couple for unity and strength during our day-to-day trials, both large and small. Help us to be steadfast. We pray we will remain strong in You amid the trials of life.

DAY 7

Desperate for the Lord

But he said to me, "My grace is sufficient for you, for my power is made perfect in weakness." Therefore I will boast all the more gladly about my weaknesses, so that Christ's power may rest on me.

2 Corinthians 12:9

The word *desperate* has a negative connotation. No one wants to be desperate for anything. It makes you sound as if you'd be willing to compromise and settle for something less. But I'd like to suggest a different meaning for this word when it comes to marriage. Couples who come to the Lord with desperation know they bring nothing to the table and must completely rely upon the Lord.

When I'm desperate for the Lord, I know I don't come with a résumé of things to brag about. I'm not prideful of my skills, and I realize my best accomplishments are like "filthy rags" to the Lord (Isa. 64:6). It keeps me at a place where I am dependent on God to be my strength and to be the source of hope in our marriage. Apart from Christ, we can do nothing (John 15:5), so we come desperate for Him to do what only He can do in our lives and in our marriages.

Paul wrote about his weaknesses in 2 Corinthians 12 when he shared about "a thorn in [his] flesh" (v. 7). In his weakness and impairment, Paul knew God's power would be made perfect in his dependence on Him. When we humbly acknowledge our need for God to be strong in our lives, we admit our need for His help and grace. While the world values strength and independence, God values a humble, desperate dependence on Him. Once again, God works in a completely different way from the world.

I remember the days when each of our four sons was a baby, completely dependent on Kristen and me for everything. The only thing they could do on their own was cry, eat, sleep, and poop. And even in those things we had to help them! Our babies needed us for everything and desperately cried out for our help.

Early in your marriage, you will more than likely struggle at some point along the way. Instead of trying to fix it on your own, be desperate and come to the Lord to help you. As a baby cries out for his or her caregivers, so you can desperately cry out to the Lord.

Lord, we need You. Every day, minute, and hour of our lives we need You. We think we can fix things all on our own, and we think our accomplishments are a big deal. But please remind us how much we need You, that we should learn to be desperate for You. Help us to remember that when we are weak and dependent, we are strong— not in our own power but in Yours.

DAY 8

Forgiving

Be kind and compassionate to one another, forgiving each other, just as in Christ God forgave you.

Ephesians 4:32

I'm writing this entry about the character trait of forgiveness on Easter Sunday. On Easter, followers of Jesus Christ celebrate the fact that Jesus took our sins upon Himself. He died on the cross for the forgiveness of our sins so that we can have a personal, intimate relationship with God the Father. The weight of all our sins was placed on Jesus, and He died for you and for me—and then rose again to give us life. When we place our faith in Jesus, God forgives us of our sins—the debt has been paid, not because of anything we've done or because we deserve it, but because of the kindness and forgiveness of the Lord.

Paul said followers of Jesus Christ are to forgive one another in the same way as God forgave us through Christ (Eph. 4:32). We're to show the same forgiveness to others as we've been shown. No relationship will provide you with more opportunities to forgive and to seek forgiveness than marriage. In both the big and small things of life, you and your significant other will humbly seek and offer forgiveness. And when you don't forgive your spouse, you're only hurting yourself and your marriage.

A few days ago, I heard a story about a couple who got divorced. The wife struggled with an addiction to alcohol, and their household, including their kids, was a total mess, largely due to the wife's addiction. When their family hit rock bottom and the couple split, the ex-wife started dealing with her addiction. As the ex-husband grew closer to Jesus, he knew the only right response was to forgive her as he was forgiven. He also took an active role in helping his ex-wife get help for her addiction through a Christ-centered twelve-step recovery program. They're now joyfully remarried, and their family has been restored. This is a beautiful picture of the gospel and shows others the hope and forgiveness of Christ.

Kristen and I make it a regular practice to ensure we're not harboring bitterness or unforgiveness against each other. We try to keep short accounts (Eph. 4:26), and we make an effort to apologize and seek forgiveness whenever one of us falls short. I've seen too many couples sweep frustrations under the rug and not deal with their issues. If you have a forgiveness problem, then there's a good chance you don't rightly understand how you've been forgiven of everything through the death of Jesus.

Lord, we pray we would be a husband and wife who are experts in forgiveness. We pray we would quickly own our struggles and seek forgiveness from one another daily. Help us to be humble, own our part, apologize, and seek forgiveness. We pray we'll be experts in forgiveness because we know how much we've been forgiven through Christ.

DAY 9

Contrite

My sacrifice, O God, is a broken spirit; a broken and contrite heart you, God, will not despise.

Psalm 51:17

Recently, my wife and I got into a short argument about our son's basketball schedule. We live in Waco, two hours from where he had a basketball tournament on a Saturday and Sunday. I got frustrated with Kristen because she wanted our son to keep his commitment even though it inconvenienced me and our family. I snapped at her and ended the conversation without resolving the issue.

I hate when I mess up with my wife. I don't like to admit when I'm wrong; my pride kicks in, and my defensiveness goes up. I can't see clearly and elevate my ego above my spouse and our marriage. God opposes proud people like me in these moments (James 4:6), and so does Kristen. During these times, I don't desire restoration and reconciliation. Instead, I just want to win and be right.

I know I'm not alone—nobody likes to be wrong, in marriage or in any relationship. We want to be right, and we don't want to admit our sins and faults. But when my heart is contrite, I can acknowledge where I fall short and do anything and everything God asks of me. I'm more willing to do what my spouse and close friends challenge me to do. Contrition is a sacrifice, because in the process we lay aside our desires and elevate our spouse above ourselves.

God wants you to be willing to do anything and everything He asks of you. He desires a "broken and contrite heart" in you (Ps. 51:17). And guess what? So does your signficant other. They want to know you're willing to admit your faults. They want to know you'll confess when you fall short and not defend yourself when you do. A broken and contrite heart leads us to feel remorse and act to bring healing to our relationship.

A marriage not marked by brokenness and contrition won't thrive and may not even survive. But one that is shows a willingness to grow, heal, and resolve conflict in a God-honoring way, laying aside selfish and prideful desires. As David said in Psalm 51:17 after his sin against the Lord and others, God will not despise a broken and contrite heart in you and your spouse.

Lord, help us to be broken and contrite in our relationship with You and with each other. Help us not to be prideful, for we know You oppose the proud but show favor and grace to the humble (James 4:6). Help us to be humble when we fall short and to embrace a broken and contrite posture, knowing that You desire this in us and in our marriage.

DAY 10

Committed

So they are no longer two, but one flesh. Therefore what God
has joined together, let no one separate.

Matthew 19:6

I don't know about you, but unless we're talking about a bag
of peanut butter M&Ms, I'm good at starting things but not
nearly as good at finishing them. I've started house projects,
diets, exercise plans, and annual goals, but I rarely seem to finish what I start. I suffer from a lack of commitment to cross
the finish line with projects. My friend Joe, on the other hand,
does an excellent job of finishing projects and helping others
complete tasks on their to-do lists.

Marriage calls us to a level of commitment rarely modeled
in our world. And unfortunately, many couples don't finish

what they start. When the going gets tough, individuals begin to look for ways out of the marriage. They distract themselves with work, hobbies, or other people, and they often quit working on their marriage. This leads to a high divorce rate and a high percentage of couples who stay married but are miserable together.

In Matthew 19:3–6, Jesus quoted Genesis 2:24 as He talked about God's design for marriage. At the end of this passage, He said, "What God has joined together, let no one separate" (v. 6). Jesus was speaking to the commitment and permanence required in marriage. While friendships and work relationships come and go, God intends marriage to be a lifelong commitment.

I'm grateful Kristen and I are committed to each other and to our marriage covenant. I don't fear rejection from her, and I don't need to wonder if she's going to run off with someone else. This type of commitment God calls for in marriage allows us to be "one flesh" with each other and to experience safety and intimacy in our relationship.

In the book of Ruth, a woman named Naomi lost her husband and her two married sons. One of her daughters-in-law was a woman named Ruth, who said to Naomi, "Where you go I will go, and where you stay I will stay. Your people will be my people and your God my God" (1:16). I admire Ruth's commitment to stay by Naomi. In marriage, God calls us to an even higher commitment to our spouse.[1]

> *Lord, thank You that Your commitment to us is not conditional upon our behavior or the decisions we make.*

We pray You'd help us to be committed unconditionally to each other in marriage and that our commitment wouldn't be based on behavior or feelings. Though we may struggle in other life commitments, help us to be radically different in our commitment to our marriage.

DAY 11

Visionary

Now to him who is able to do immeasurably more than all we ask or imagine, according to his power that is at work within us, to him be glory in the church and in Christ Jesus throughout all generations, for ever and ever! Amen.

Ephesians 3:20–21

A good friend of mine often talks about what to do when you're not where you want to be in life. It's a simple process: first, identify where you are today and then figure out where you want to be in the future. Next, come up with a plan to get yourself there. For example, let's say I weigh 250 pounds but want to weigh 225 pounds. I know where I am today (250) and where I want to be in a year (225), so I come up with a plan to help me get there.

This same principle works in marriage. Even though you can't measure your marriage on an objective scale, you can think through where you are in your relationship today and where you want to be down the road. This process helps you realize you can grow and improve in your relationship. You can take steps to become more like Christ and to help you better love and serve your spouse. A husband and wife who are visionary will take steps to strengthen and grow their marriage.

In Ephesians 3:20–21, Paul prayed to the God "who is able to do immeasurably more than all we ask or imagine." Paul had great vision for what the Lord could do in every part of his life. His prayer acknowledged the infinite riches and power of the Lord. This very God can do more than any of us can imagine.

What if you and your future spouse had a vision for your marriage that lived up to Paul's prayer? What if you prayed for God to grow your marriage beyond your dreams? If you did, I think you'd gain a vision for an extraordinary marriage.

Kristen and I have a vision for our marriage to honor the Lord. We often pray for our children to walk with Jesus for the rest of their lives. We want to use our gifts of teaching and hospitality to lead and serve others, and we want to use our home to engage with Christians and non-Christians.

I encourage you and your significant other to have big dreams for your marriage and for your lives together as husband and wife. There's no doubt He can do it.

God, today we're going to pray Your very words right back to You for our marriage. Because we know You can do "immeasurably more than all we ask or imagine" (Eph. 3:20), we pray You would use Your power that is at work within us and that You would get all the glory in the church and through Your Son, Jesus, throughout all generations, forever and ever.

DAY 12

Kingdom-Minded

And he died for all, that those who live should no longer live for
themselves but for him who died for them and was raised again.

2 Corinthians 5:15

When I think back on many of my days, I see I've made dozens
of decisions based on what benefits me most. Today, I got up
at 5:00 a.m. so I could have some quiet time to read my Bible,
pray, journal, and work out. Then I made a pot of coffee (for
me), made some oatmeal (for me), took a shower (for others!),
listened to the podcasts I wanted to listen to, and worked.

If we're honest, we'll admit that most of us tend to seek
our own comfort and pleasure. This is only natural, since our
culture values comfort and pleasure. That doesn't mean we're
all selfish losers who think only of ourselves. But how much of

our lives do we live for the One who died and was raised for our sake (2 Cor. 5:15)?

Most of the decisions we make that benefit only ourselves never really satisfy us. At some point we realize we must live for something greater. In his book *A Lifelong Love*, pastor Gary Thomas said, "Marriages without a magnificent obsession are racing toward boredom. It's only a matter of time."[1]

What if you and your future spouse lived with a "magnificent obsession"? What if the decisions you made in marriage weren't just for your own pleasure and comfort but for the benefit of the kingdom of God? When we rightly realize that Jesus Christ died and was raised for us, it changes the way we look at all of life. It motivates us to live for His glory and the good of others.

When your marriage is kingdom-minded, you look beyond your own benefits and seek to introduce people to Jesus. You make decisions together out of your love for the Lord and others. At times you will even sacrifice your short-term pleasure and comfort for the sake of the long-term benefit of others.

Imagine what our marriages, churches, and communities would be like if we chose to live for the One who died for us and to be kingdom-minded in all we do as husband and wife.

God, we pray You would help us live with a "magnificent obsession" for You and Your glory. We pray our marriage would be kingdom-minded. Help us break free from the kingdom of self and our tendency to focus on our own comfort and pleasure. We need Your help in this, and we pray our marriage would be different from the marriages of the world.

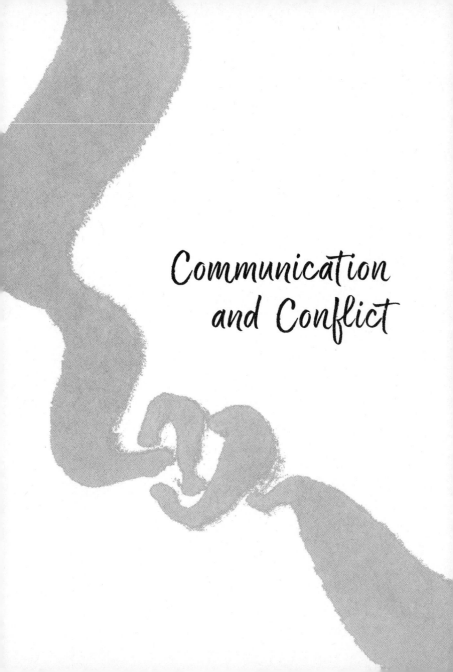

Communication
and Conflict

DAY 13

Repentant

I tell you that in the same way there will be more rejoicing in heaven over one sinner who repents than over ninety-nine righteous persons who do not need to repent.

Luke 15:7

Every one of us knows what it's like to struggle with a specific sin and feel like we can never overcome it. We feel bad about what we've done, confess to falling short, and promise never to do it again. We do well for a while, face temptation, and the cycle repeats itself. It could be a struggle with porn, drinking or overeating, spending in excess, or any number of things.

When we repent of a sin struggle, we confess to God and agree with Him that we need to change our behavior and turn back to the Lord. It's an active process of asking God for forgiveness and turning away from our sin. Since all of us sin and fall short of the glory of God (Rom. 3:23), every follower of Christ should be familiar with confession and repentance. In Luke 15:7, Jesus said there is great rejoicing when we repent of sin and turn toward Him.

In marriage, you get the opportunity to confess your sins to your spouse. When you confess your sins to each other, you both receive the opportunity to heal. When you are married, you will get the privilege and blessing of doing this with your spouse on a daily, ongoing basis. You get the honor and challenge of helping the other become more like Jesus Christ. When your spouse confesses to you and seeks forgiveness, you play a key role in helping your spouse understand what it means to repent and walk away from sin.

I'm deeply grateful for all the ways Kristen has helped me repent of my sin struggles over the years. I have confessed and repented of struggles with overeating, anger, people-pleasing, and so much more. Kristen partners with me in addressing my sin and turning to the Lord to help me become more like Jesus Christ. I seek to do the same for her. For this reason, it's crucial for you and your future spouse to learn how to repent of your sins and battle them together.

Lord, thank You for the forgiveness of sins. Thank You that Your Son, Jesus Christ, died for our sins and took our sins upon Himself. And thank You that Your Spirit dwells inside us to convict us of our sin. Help us not just to confess our sin but to turn back toward You. And please help us to partner together well in marriage to become more holy.

DAY 14

Approachable

Come to me, all you who are weary and burdened, and I will give you rest.

Matthew 11:28

What do you do when you're stressed or need comfort? How about when you need to confess sin—where do you turn? Do you feel safe and secure approaching your significant other? I hope you would be willing and able to go to them when you need help, when you want to celebrate, and when you need to confess.

No one in the history of the world has been more approachable or safer than Jesus Christ. We see this in Matthew 11:28 when Jesus told His followers to come to Him and He would give them rest. Even though Jesus knows every thought we've ever had and every sin we've ever committed, He still promises rest to those who come to Him. He provides a safe place for us when we're stressed, exhausted, and everything in between.

Your spouse should be the safest relationship for you on this planet. Ideally, when you are married, you can be naked without shame with your spouse (Gen. 2:25). You don't need to fear their response. They won't reject you; instead, they'll fight for you, alongside you. You'll "carry each other's burdens" (Gal. 6:2), and you'll seek wisdom. Your spouse should be a gift to you as you approach them with any and every thing.

I've worked with couples who take advantage of the weaknesses of their spouse. They use their confessions against them and mock them in their struggles. This is the exact opposite of a one-flesh relationship (Gen. 2:24). When you see your marriage and spouse rightly, you realize they're one flesh with you. What hurts your spouse hurts you, and vice versa.

What if your relationship proved to be safe and your spouse secure? What if you could run to your spouse to celebrate your wins and cry with each other in your losses? I want this for you, and more important, God wants it for you.

God, thank You that we can come to You and You will give us rest. Thank You for not rejecting us in our trials and for welcoming us with open arms. We pray that we would act the same way in our marriage, that we wouldn't blame and point the finger at each other but rather be approachable and safe for each other to come to in the goods and bads of life.

DAY 15

Slow to Anger

My dear brothers and sisters, take note of this: Everyone should be quick to listen, slow to speak and slow to become angry, because human anger does not produce the righteousness that God desires.

James 1:19–20

One of my biggest challenges from a young age has been a quick temper. I used to get angry easily when watching my favorite teams on TV. And when I work too much and don't get enough sleep, I become quick to get angry at coworkers, friends, and even my family. I know I'm not alone; I see this tendency toward anger in many other Christians.

James gave us a great challenge—that we would be "slow to become angry" (1:19). A person who is slow to become angry is much more pleasant to be with and typically makes for a better spouse. James also explained that intense, sustained anger doesn't help us become more like Christ, and it doesn't make us more righteous.

One of the challenges you and your significant other will face in marriage is unmet expectations. Sometimes you'll be unaware that you have expectations of your spouse, and you may become frustrated when your spouse doesn't act the way you want them to. Other times your expectations will be known to yourself but unspoken, and you may get frustrated with your spouse when you hold them to an expectation they're unaware of. And at other times, your expectations will be completely unrealistic. When your spouse doesn't live up to these unrealistic expectations, you may get angry with them.

How can you become a spouse who is slow to anger?

- *Ask God to help you become more patient.* Ask Him to lengthen your patience and help you be slow to anger.
- *Memorize Bible verses about patience.* The Bible is filled with verses about becoming slow to anger (Prov. 14:29; 15:1; 19:11; Eph. 4:26; James 1:19–20).
- *Follow God's example.* Take note of how God is slow to anger and abounding in love (Exod. 34:6; Ps. 103:8; 145:8). Become more like the Lord, and He'll take care of the rest!

God, it's so easy at times for many of us to lose our tempers. We tend to get frustrated when things don't go our way, we hold our partner to standards we don't keep ourselves, and we can take our internal frustrations out on others. Help us to become slow to anger. Help us to let go of unrealistic expectations and learn to be patient, understanding, and gracious when things don't go our way. We pray our relationship will be one marked by patience and understanding.

DAY 16

Wholesome in Talk

Do not let any unwholesome talk come out of your mouths, but only what is helpful for building others up according to their needs, that it may benefit those who listen.

Ephesians 4:29

In Ephesians 4:29, Paul made his point abundantly clear: "Do not let *any* unwholesome talk come out of your mouths." He didn't say we can let *some* unwholesome talk come out of our mouths. He didn't make allowances for angry words, cussing, or slander. I may argue or try to make excuses, but Paul simply didn't allow it.

In marriage, we're challenged by Paul to allow only wholesome, uplifting talk to come from our mouths. Marriage will provide you and your future spouse with plenty of opportunities to gossip, speak with sarcasm, or complain. You may be tempted to cuss when angry or in quoting a movie or a friend. All the above have been consistent challenges for me. As a premarried couple, you may doubt you or your future spouse would use words in ways that tear each other down, but when you get married, you will face challenges every single day in your words.

The world will do all it can to tear you and your spouse down. Coworkers, neighbors, and family members may be experts in unwholesome talk. But you will have the opportunity to stand out and be unique. You can use your words to build up your spouse instead of tearing them down. I've found asking myself, *Is what I'm about to say going to tear someone down or build them up?* to be a relationship-changing question. If you run this question by everything about to come out of your mouth, it will change your marriage.

Here are a few quick suggestions on how to do this well:

- *Be careful of sarcasm.* Some of us may resort to sarcasm to get quick and easy laughs from others. However, a sarcastic comment can tear others down (Prov. 26:18–19). Ask your significant other if you're sarcastic on occasion, and if so, ask them to help you choose your words wisely.
- *Don't be a gossip.* Many people thrive on sharing juicy gossp. We "spill the tea" because it makes others think we have inside information. But gossip tears others down instead of building them up (26:22).
- *Watch what you watch.* Choose entertainment that isn't filled with bad language (Eph. 5:4).

- *Spend time with encouragers.* Surround yourself with friends who lift up and encourage with their words (Prov. 13:20).

Your marriage can be so different from the marriages of so many around you. All it takes is choosing to be wholesome in your speech instead of slandering, gossiping, or tearing each other down.

God, help us to follow Your example in how You use words to lift up and encourage. We need Your help so that the words that come out of our mouths are wholesome. May our marriage be filled with words marked by blessing and life, not discouragement and death. In moments when we're tempted to cuss, slander, gossip, and tear down, please help us be wholesome in everything we say.

DAY 17

Gracious

For it is by grace you have been saved, through faith—and this is not from yourselves, it is the gift of God—not by works, so that no one can boast.

Ephesians 2:8–9

What's more important and central to the Christian life than the grace of God? In His infinite grace, God gave us the greatest gift we could ever get, at no cost to us. While *mercy* can be defined as not getting something you deserve, *grace* can be defined as getting something you don't deserve. Because of our sin, each of us deserves eternal separation from God. We deserve punishment and justice for our sins.

In His grace, God placed that punishment on His Son, Jesus. Justice was served on the cross. And you and I receive the free gift of salvation through faith in Jesus's finished work on the cross and through the grace of the Father. We've received G.R.A.C.E.—God's Riches At Christ's Expense.

As followers of Jesus Christ, our aim is to be like Him and to emulate His life and attributes. Therefore, we ought to demonstrate grace toward others, especially toward our spouse. In marriage, you will come across countless opportunities to receive grace from your spouse and to offer grace to your spouse—to give them something they don't deserve.

- You will forget to do something you promised your spouse you'd do—and instead of getting frustrated with you, they bring you breakfast in bed. *Grace*.
- You will be stuck in an important meeting at work and come home later than you promised—and instead of pouting, your spouse makes you a candlelight dinner complete with your favorite flowers. *Grace*.
- You'll be short with your spouse one evening—and instead of matching or even escalating your response, your spouse affirms you and tells you how much they love you. *Grace*.

A Christian marriage gives us opportunities to demonstrate the grace of Jesus Christ, all day every day. Let us never forget His work on the cross, and may we also never forget the unending, saving grace of God.

> *God, thank You for Your grace—Your riches at the expense of Your Son's life. No quantity or quality of good*

deeds could ever be enough to earn Your favor. We all have gone astray, yet You paid the price through Your Son, Jesus Christ, and You offer us salvation, something we could never earn. Thank You for the grace that provides eternal life to all those who put their faith in Jesus. Help us to be a gracious husband and wife.

DAY 18

Gentle

A gentle answer turns away wrath, but a harsh word stirs up anger.

Proverbs 15:1

I love when the book of Proverbs provides a clear contrast between two behaviors. Proverbs 15:1 says when we're harsh with our spouse, we will stir up anger. And "human anger does not produce the righteousness that God desires" (James 1:20). But when we're gentle, we turn away wrath and invite a conversation and a more intimate relationship.

In marriage, you and your spouse will have many opportunities either to stir up anger or turn away wrath. And every time, you will need to choose a gentle answer so that you can build your relationship. For many of us, our natural—and often easier—response is to react with anger. Candidly, this is a fleshly response that typically happens when we're not controlled by the Holy Spirit.

Gentleness marks my youngest son. When I watch him interact with his friends, I see his gentle nature shine through. He's kind and loveable, and he exhibits the fruit of the Spirit in his gentleness (Gal. 5:22–23). He's never met a stranger, and his smile and kindness inspire me. Last year, we went on a father-son trip to San Diego, and he waved at every car that drove by and said hello to everyone we passed on the street. When I watch my son's gentle spirit toward others, I see how it builds his relationships with others and how it will benefit his future marriage (assuming he gets married).

Sometimes when we see people who are gentle, we think they are weak and lack strength and conviction. Yet we know Jesus is gentle and doesn't lack in any of these attributes. In Matthew 11:29, He described Himself as "gentle and humble in heart." If Jesus is gentle, then gentleness is a trait we should all strive for.

Your marriage should be a safe place for you and your spouse to grow and be honest and open with each other. Harsh words lead others to shut down, while gentle words invite restoration and relationship.

God, help us to be gentle in every way with each other. Help us to turn away wrath and not stir up anger. We pray that we'd exhibit gentleness as evidence of the fruit of the Holy Spirit and that our lives would be increasingly marked by gentleness. When our natural tendency is to be harsh, help our lives to be marked by the gentleness of our Savior. Thank You for Your gentleness toward us every moment of our lives.

DAY 19

Listening

Fools find no pleasure in understanding but delight in airing their own opinions.

Proverbs 18:2

I believe in the importance of every single trait discussed in this prayer guide. A prayerful application of each of these attributes will help strengthen your relationship with Jesus, your spouse's relationship with Jesus, and your marriage. But some traits seem to be more important than others in leading to a thriving marriage. For this reason, pay careful attention to this: don't be a fool in your relationship.

The writer of Proverbs 18:2 rightly provided a contrast that will serve your marriage well if applied but lead to challenges if ignored: a foolish spouse takes no pleasure in understanding their spouse but delights in expressing their own opinions. In other words, a foolish spouse doesn't care what their spouse thinks or feels. A foolish spouse wants only to win the argument and prove they're right (and their spouse is wrong). Instead of being quick to listen and slow to speak (James 1:19), a foolish spouse chooses to be quick to speak and slow to listen to their spouse.

When you are married, there will likely be days when you don't want to listen to your spouse. They'll annoy you and frustrate you and try every ounce of your patience. You'll be confident you're right and they're wrong. But the goal in marriage is rarely, if ever, to win and to be right. As we have seen, in marriage you and your spouse "become one flesh" (Gen. 2:24), meaning that a loss for your spouse is a loss for you, and a win for your spouse is a win for you. It's a paradigm-shifting mentality that will help strengthen the marital bond when you seek not to win but to understand.

In fact, the goal of communication should be mutual understanding. When this happens, you both clearly communicate your needs and desires, and each spouse fully understands what the other is communicating. Listening is essential to get to this place in your marriage.

A few suggestions:

- *Give your spouse your full attention.* Put down your phone and listen to your future spouse.
- *Say it back.* Repeat back to them what you heard so your spouse knows you're listening.
- *Work hard at listening!* This doesn't come naturally to many of us, so we need to intentionally work on listening instead of playing the fool.

Fools don't thrive in marriage. Be wise and choose to delight in listening to your future spouse instead of simply expressing your own opinions.

Lord, help us to be wise and to delight in understanding each other. Help us to put each other's desires before our own, and please help us lay aside our drive to win. Help us to communicate with each other like the wise and not like the fool. And help us to keep our mouths closed when it's time to focus on listening to and understanding our partner.

DAY 20

Encouraging

But encourage one another daily, as long as it is called "Today,"
so that none of you may be hardened by sin's deceitfulness.

Hebrews 3:13

I don't know if you've noticed, but life is filled with strife—financial, relational, spiritual, and so much more. Every aspect of life is marked by sin and difficulty. If we're not careful, these challenges can make us cynical. The writer of Hebrews said we need to be careful that we don't become hardened by these trials, and we need daily encouragement. Most of us are quick to criticize and critique but are much slower to encourage.

Marriage provides you with a unique opportunity to wake up and fall asleep next to your spouse every day. Who better to provide them daily encouragement both morning and night than you? God gives you the amazing privilege of encouraging your spouse daily as you get to help them battle the deceitfulness of sin.

What can it look like to encourage your spouse? Encouragement is one of my strongest gifts, so I'll share a few ways I've done this over our twenty-plus years of marriage.

- *Send a personalized text to your future spouse.* Be specific with your encouragement. For example, don't just say, "You're amazing!" Say, "The way you cared for your friend today showed me how much you love others and consider them more important than yourself."
- *Write encouraging notes.* Leave sticky notes on the steering wheel, in their Bible, on the bathroom mirror. Write down an inside joke or tell them you're praying for them.
- *Share a Bible verse.* Nothing encourages us more than comfort and truth from God's Word. Share a verse with your future spouse, reminding them of the goodness of God.
- *Pray for them.* Pray for your spouse in person and when you're away from them. Pray God would help their heart not be hardened by sin.

You can put this into practice today. Text, call, or pray for your significant other, and specifically encourage them with something God-honoring you see in them. So often we wait and think we'll get to it later. If you wait, often you'll forget. Encourage them today!

Heavenly Father, thank You for the truth of Your Word and for the body of Christ. Thank You that You don't leave us alone but give us Your Word, Spirit, and people to encourage us. We pray that our marriage will be marked by Christlike encouragement and that we will be a husband and wife who encourage each other so that we're not hardened by the deceitfulness of sin.

Spiritual
Intimacy

DAY 21

Biblical

They are like a man building a house, who dug down deep and laid the foundation on rock. When a flood came, the torrent struck that house but could not shake it, because it was well built.

Luke 6:48

This is one of the most important days of prayer in this book. Every day's trait and prayer is important, but this one might be the most foundational. I've stopped to pray for you several times because I so badly want you to build your life and your marriage on the right foundation. The world will try to pull you in so many different directions. But my hope is that you and your significant other will dig down deep and build your lives on the solid-rock foundation of Jesus Christ.

The one guarantee we see in Luke 6:46–49 is that storms will come in our lives. Whether it's financial hardships, difficult in-laws, job issues, infertility, a pornography struggle, or something else, you will face challenges as a married couple. The question is how you'll respond when the storms hit. Will your life stand firm like the house built on the rock in verse 48, or crash down like the house built on sand in verse 49?

What does it look like to have a biblical marriage?

- *A biblical marriage seeks counsel from God's Word.* Both husband and wife are students of the Bible.
- *A biblical marriage obeys God's Word.* Both spouses know what God's Word says and do what it says.
- *A biblical marriage seeks counsel.* The husband and wife go to other faithful followers of Jesus when they are stuck and need counsel. This could be a trusted friend, pastor, or biblical counselor or therapist.
- *A biblical marriage is based on truth.* Spouses consistently remind themselves of biblical truth and fight back together against culture's picture and definition of marriage.
- *A biblical marriage is Christ-honoring.* Each spouse takes consistent steps to become more and more like Jesus Christ.

In short, I hope you continue to build your life and marriage on Jesus Christ. Yes, troubles will come into your life, but the home—and marriage—that is built on a deep, solid foundation will stand through all trials that may come your way.

Lord, there are often days when we don't want to do the hard work to become like You. We'd rather watch TV than read our Bibles. We'd rather sleep in on a Sunday morning. And we'd rather keep our money for ourselves. But what we really want is a biblical marriage. Help us to become the godly husband and wife You want us to be. Please help us to be more dependent on You than on anything or anyone else so that we may build our marriage on Your strong foundation.

DAY 22

Disciplined

Like a city whose walls are broken through is a person who lacks self-control.

Proverbs 25:28

One of the most consistent lessons I've learned in my years of ministry is the importance of being disciplined. Whether it's daily time in God's Word, a consistent exercise routine, or a habit of daily prayer (like I hope you're cultivating through this book), it's hard to overestimate the essential significance of discipline. A person who lacks self-control will lose the battles of life. Proverbs 25:28 says they will become like a city under attack whose walls are destroyed.

Adam Grant, an organizational psychologist and professor at Wharton School of Business, once said, "The seeds of greatness are planted in the daily grind."[1] To become great at anything in life, we need to become experts in the disciplines of the daily grind. This principle holds true for individuals and for marriages. Every couple needs to be disciplined in daily planting seeds of greatness. This discipline allows couples to thrive.

The tough part about discipline is that most of us don't want to be disciplined in our lifestyle. I know I'd rather watch TV and sleep than exercise or even pray with my wife. But it helps to remember that choices you and I make today can have an impact for years to come, especially if we consistently make the same healthy choices.

What does it look like for a couple to be disciplined? Here are a few examples. A disciplined couple will

- *make time every day to communicate with each other.* Keep short accounts when conflict or disagreements arise.
- *spend time with each other.* Go on date nights on a consistent basis to help keep romance alive.
- *make confession a regular practice in marriage.* You and your spouse will have countless opportunities to ask for and grant forgiveness.
- *look for ways to serve each other.* Each spouse joyfully does chores and tasks around the house because they know it serves their spouse well.

In 1 Timothy 4:7, Paul said we are to "train [ourselves] to be godly." When we train we must be disciplined—it's worth the work to become more like the Lord!

Heavenly Father, we pray we would be disciplined in life and in marriage. Help us to do the things that keep us close to You and to each other. We confess at times we don't want to be disciplined—we want to do what we want to do! Help us when we don't feel like it, and thank You for grace whenever we fall short. Thank You that Your love for us is not contingent on how disciplined or undisciplined we are. May Your grace and love for us always amaze us.

DAY 23

Faithful

For the word of the LORD is right and true; he is faithful in all he does.

Psalm 33:4

One big difference between you, your significant other, every other human being on the planet, and the God of the universe is that He is faithful and the rest of us are not. Sure, there will be times when you will be full of faith, but there will be many times when you're not. At times, you will forget how good God is, and you will forget what He's done. God, on the other hand, is always faithful (2 Tim. 2:13). To be faithful means that you will be true to your word and commitments. As I mentioned earlier, the goal of this book is not just for you to be a better future spouse. More than anything, I hope you and your significant other will both become more like Jesus Christ. And the best chance you have of being a great spouse and having a great marriage is for you to become more and more like Jesus—every day of your life on this planet. To that end, I encourage you to pray that you'd be faithful, because Jesus is faithful.

When we think of being faithful in terms of marriage, we tend to assume it means the individual is not cheating on their spouse or having an affair. While this is certainly part of what it means to be a faithful spouse, there's much more to being faithful than just not cheating on your spouse.

I had more trouble choosing a verse for faithfulness than for any other trait in this book because the Bible is filled with verses describing the faithfulness of the Lord. All God's promises to Israel were fulfilled (Josh. 21:45). Faithfulness is among the fruit of the Spirit (Gal. 5:22–23). The God who calls us is faithful, and He will do what He says He's going to do (1 Thess. 5:24).

Here's why faithfulness is important: In marriage, you and your spouse will let each other down time and time again. You'll be disappointed in your spouse, and you may even question their love for God and for you at times. They're going to forget to do something you've asked them to do. They're going to make promises and not keep them. They're going to choose work, TV, friends, or kids over you at times. And guess what? You will do the same. I want to remind you that neither of you are perfect, and you both will make mistakes.

To that end, keep your eyes on Jesus, the One who is always faithful. He remains faithful even on your least faithful days.

Thank You, Lord, that You are always faithful. You do what You say You're going to do, and we're grateful for Your faithful love for us. We're not always faithful, so please help us to become more and more like You, to be faithful as You are faithful. Please help us to be faithful to each other in marriage. Thank You for always being who You are and for always doing what You say You'll do.

DAY 24

Abiding

I am the vine; you are the branches. If you remain in me and
I in you, you will bear much fruit; apart from me you can do
nothing.

John 15:5

There might not be a churchier word than *abide*. In the churches
I've served in, whenever a question comes up in small groups
regarding conflict or big decisions, the solution often seems
to be that we should "abide." What does it mean to abide in
Christ, and why does it matter in a Christian marriage? As
you get ready to say "I do," why should you care about what it
means to be abiding?

To answer this question, let's look closer at John 15:5. Jesus
said we will bear fruit only if we remain in Christ. What does

it mean to bear fruit? It's not like we're trees that make apples or oranges! When Jesus said we will "bear much fruit," He meant living in a way that shows evidence of a relationship with Himself. This means staying in a dependent relationship with Him.

It also means we won't produce any fruit and instead will wither away if we're not dependent on Him and don't abide. We must learn from Christ and be with Him through His Word and prayer. We know the way to become more like Jesus Christ is to spend time with Him and realize nothing good ultimately happens apart from Him.

In this passage, Jesus was talking to His disciples on His final night with them before He was crucified. He told them how they could grow in their relationship with Him. Because He was about to die, Jesus wanted to make it abundantly clear how His followers would develop in becoming more like Him. He let them know that apart from Him, they could do nothing. Not something, not a few things, but *nothing*. You will not be able to grow in any of the ways discussed and prayed about in this book unless you abide with Christ.

Pray that you will be an abiding spouse. Much of life will try to pull you offsides and away from the Lord: busyness, money, other people, technology, and so much more. If you don't make your relationship with the Lord the most integral, essential part of your life, you will lack the fundamental trait you need to be a godly husband or wife. If you and your future spouse are going to grow closer to the Lord and to each other, you need to abide in Christ.

God, we want to become more like You. Help us to see the only way to grow spiritually is by abiding in You all day, every day. Help us learn from You and spend time with You through Your Word and prayer. Show us how we can love and serve each other through an intimate, abiding relationship with You. And help us to abide in Christ all the days of our lives as a married couple.

DAY 25

Loyal

Know therefore that the LORD your God is God; he is the faithful God, keeping his covenant of love to a thousand generations of those who love him and keep his commandments.

Deuteronomy 7:9

I'm so grateful God is loyal to us. Even though we sin against Him, neglect our relationship with Him at times, and often choose ourselves over Him and others, He remains loyal to followers of Jesus Christ. As human beings, we tend to be fickle. When someone offends or frustrates us, we turn away from them. Work relationships end, friendships change, and marriages and families suffer. But not so with God. He remains loyal to His children.

As followers of Christ, we're to be like Him. We're to follow His example and "be imitators of God" (Eph. 5:1 ESV). This means we're to be loyal to our spouse in marriage. As God is loyal to us in our ups and downs, we're to be loyal to our spouse in our relational ups and downs. When you get married, you and your spouse become one flesh (Gen. 2:24), which means you fight for unity and loyalty.

What does loyalty look like in marriage?

- *You put your marriage before yourself.* When you say "I do," you no longer think only of your individual self; you think of your marriage and family above yourself.
- *You help your spouse use their gifts.* You work to ensure each other's success and do all you can to help your spouse use their gifts for God's glory and the good of others.
- *You run toward tough conversations instead of ignoring them.* Time won't heal wounds or marital problems. You must communicate with your spouse instead of ignoring them or running away.
- *You give each other honest feedback and support.* In a healthy marriage, you should be able to tell your spouse anything and everything. You also choose to believe the best and not assume the worst.
- *You give your spouse the gift of your time.* Your marriage is the most important human relationship you have on the planet.
- *You maintain a long-term perspective.* You choose to function at this level for the long haul, not just for short seasons of time.

When you're loyal, you're committed to doing all you can to help your spouse become more and more like Jesus Christ. What a gift!

> *Lord, our world is marked by a lack of loyalty. When the going gets tough, people quit. They run away from problems and from people. God, help us to be loyal to You and to each other. Thank You that You model this loyalty perfectly. Thank You that Your Son, Jesus, remained loyal to us, to the point of death on the cross. Help us to be imitators of You in every way.*

DAY 26

God-Fearing

The fear of the LORD is the beginning of wisdom, and knowledge of the Holy One is understanding.

Proverbs 9:10

Most of us don't take our sin seriously enough. I know at times I can abuse grace and, knowing that God has forgiven me, I willingly choose to sin. In my mind, it's nothing big—maybe a small lie, a second glance in which I know I'm giving in to lust, or using my words to tear others down. Whenever I choose lapses like these, I'm essentially admitting I don't fear God.

The fear of God is a necessary trait for individuals and marriages. The phrase *God-fearing* does not mean being afraid of God or living in terror that He's going to hurt us or punish us. To be *God-fearing* means having reverence, awe, and respect for God.

It means we love the Lord and want to honor Him, and when we sin, we're sad we didn't obey the One who fully loves us. When we fear God, we find our hope and identity in Him.

If we don't fear God, then we probably fear the world. We often look for identity and hope in things of the world or in people. We then become a slave to the approval of others. In Galatians 1:10, Paul said, "Am I now trying to win the approval of human beings, or of God? Or am I trying to please people? If I were still trying to please people, I would not be a servant of Christ." Together as a couple, you and your significant other must decide if you're going to fear God or fear other people.

I want to appeal to you to follow God. The writer of Proverbs 9 said, "The fear of the LORD is the beginning of wisdom" (v. 10). This is your starting place. This is how you grow in your relationship with the Lord, which will allow you to grow in your relationship with each other. It all begins by living your life on the right foundation with the right fears.

Most of our lives we run from fear. But a God-fearing marriage is worthy of your full pursuit as a couple.

Lord, we often seek the praise and accolades of humans more than we seek You. Help us not to seek the approval of others but rather rest in the fact that You already approve of us because of the work of Your Son, Jesus Christ. Help us to fear You all the days of our lives as a couple. Thank You for being completely worthy of our fear and awe.

DAY 27

Worshipful

You alone are the LORD. You made the heavens, even the highest heavens, and all their starry host, the earth and all that is on it, the seas and all that is in them. You give life to everything, and the multitudes of heaven worship you.

Nehemiah 9:6

A worshipful marriage has nothing to do with whether you and your future spouse raise your hands in church during praise and worship. It has nothing to do with the style of music you like. It doesn't matter how great your significant other's voice is and whether they sing in the choir. Rather, it has everything to do with who and what you and your future spouse worship.

We all worship something or someone. Maybe it's your favorite sports team—take a look at college football fans in the fall, and you'll know exactly what I mean. Or maybe it's your favorite musician. I remember seeing a video of fans crying, screaming, and clawing their way toward a famous musician just so they could touch his shirt. It could be your bank account, your social media following, or your precious car. We are made to worship. We just often get the object of our worship wrong.

The Scriptures are filled with passages encouraging us to worship the Lord. The psalms are especially packed with calls to worship God. Yet our hearts are easily pulled offsides to worship the things of this world. To be honest, we don't visibly see God in front of us, so instead we tend to worship things we can see, touch, smell, hear, and taste. Maybe this is why God consistently reminds us in His Word why we should worship Him and Him alone.

In marriage, you and your spouse will be faced with many distractions. You must choose which ones you'll entertain and which ones you'll ignore. Anything that pulls you away from worshiping God should be left behind. This will help you keep your focus on the main thing and allow you and your spouse to build your lives on the right foundation. Everyone faces this challenge—you face it as a single person, and you'll face it in marriage.

This is a great time for you and your significant other to discuss a few questions with each other:

- Where will we go to church on Sundays?
- Do we see our everyday lives as a spiritual act of worship (Rom. 12:1)?
- If someone examined our lives, what would they say we worship most?

When it comes to worship, you'll want to get this one right and be on the same page together.

> God, we want to worship You with gladness and sing joyful songs to You. Help us to worship You and You alone and not to be distracted by the stuff of this world. Help us to be united in this pursuit so that we both equally desire to worship You in every way. We feel like we're often so easily pulled offsides to worship ourselves or stuff. We need You, every minute of every day, to help us worship You with our heart, soul, mind, and strength (Mark 12:30).

DAY 28

Prayerful

Then Jesus told his disciples a parable to show them that they
should always pray and not give up.

Luke 18:1

Do you want to be a man or woman of prayer? When spouses
pray together, they commune with the Father and ask the Holy
Spirit to compel and drive them toward intimacy with the Lord
and with each other. It's one of the most foundational habits
of our lives.

In Luke 18:1–8, Jesus told a parable about a persistent widow
who kept pleading with a judge as she sought justice regarding
an adversary. Instead of shutting her off completely, the judge
finally granted her justice. Jesus said the point of this parable
was to encourage His followers that "they should always pray
and not give up" (v. 1).

As we have seen, you are about to become one flesh with your spouse when you get married (Gen. 2:24). You will need all the prayer and help from the Father you can get! Marriage comes with challenges (1 Cor. 7:28), and believers have an enemy who would love to take down Christian marriages (1 Pet. 5:8). We can learn a lot from this persistent widow.

Speaker and author Jackie Hill Perry shared the following in an Instagram post: "So then, to become more prayerful, we have to be honest. Literally embracing the reality that we are perpetually needy even when it doesn't feel like it."[1]

I pray you and your significant other will be "perpetually needy" in your relationship, and will be humble and acknowledge your dependence on the Lord. We need to fight back against self-sufficiency.

In the introduction to this book I discussed a traffic light analogy to help guide you in your relationship. If you are a person of prayer and your significant other is not, you may take this as a sign that you either have some work to do (yellow light), or this person isn't God's provision for you (red light). I want you to be equally yoked (2 Cor. 6:14), chasing after and seeking the Father together. Pray that your eyes would be opened to see whether your relationship is facing a green, yellow, or red light.

Lord, we need You. Help us to be a couple who comes to you and prays continually, as Paul said in 1 Thessalonians 5:17. Help us to live a lifestyle of prayer, acknowledging that You never tire of us coming to You. Thank You for being the one true God and for encouraging us never to stop praying and never to quit coming to You.

Understanding Your Spouse

DAY 29

Optimistic

Because of the LORD's great love we are not consumed, for his compassions never fail. They are new every morning; great is your faithfulness.

Lamentations 3:22–23

Some days when I get home from work, I'm exhausted and worn out. After a full day of counseling people who have broken relationships with their spouse or kids, I'm often discouraged and lack hope in humanity. There's so much brokenness in our world that it's easy to fall into a pessimistic view of life. At times, all this brokenness can lead people to question the goodness of God.

In the book of Lamentations, the prophet Jeremiah reflected on the fall of God's people to foreign invasion. He grieved for

the pain and consequences the people were walking through because of their sin. In Lamentations 3:18, he said, "My splendor
is gone and all that I had hoped from the LORD." Jeremiah had
lost hope and was depressed.

But everything changed when Jeremiah remembered the
steadfast love of the Lord. He changed his perspective by no
longer looking at the world around him to define his mood and
outlook. Instead, he remembered the steadfast, compassionate,
faithful love of the Lord (vv. 22–23). There's a lot we can learn
from Jeremiah.

I can sometimes be a "glass half empty" kind of guy. And
when I am, I'm no fun to be around. I grumble, whine, and
complain, and no one wants to be with me, let alone be married
to me. My wife, Kristen, on the other hand, doesn't get fazed by
much! She usually sees the bright side of every situation. When
we choose to remember God's steadfast love, His never-failing
compassion, and His great faithfulness, everything changes.
It doesn't mean the problems go away, but our perspective of
them changes completely.

As you think ahead to your future marriage, are you filled
with hope or with despair? When a husband and wife hold an
optimistic view of life and marriage, there is always hope, even
in the darkest and most challenging days.

This is a good time to evaluate your outlook. Would you
want to be married to someone like you? How about your future
spouse—do they tend to be a pessimist or an optimist? Again,
just because you're an optimist does not mean the challenges of
the world go away. But when your perspective changes and you
look to the Lord, He fills you with hope for today and tomorrow.

> *Lord, help us to be an optimistic couple. Help us to hope in You and to find our joy in You. Thank You that You hear us. We see the pain and challenges of the world, but we need Your help to see the ups and downs of life through a different lens. Thank You for Your love, compassion, and faithfulness. May it change everything about the way we look at life.*

DAY 30

Humble

God opposes the proud but shows favor to the humble.

James 4:6

Humility can be difficult to define, but we know it when we see it—and we know when we don't see it. A person of humility thinks rightly about themselves. They don't think too highly or lowly of themselves, and they don't think about themselves too often.

The humble spouse sees themselves as God sees them. Because God sent His only Son to die for us, we know we have value. At the same time, we need to "think of [ourselves] with sober judgment," knowing we are not God (Rom. 12:3). In fact, the basic requirement of a saving faith in Jesus is humility, in that we need to acknowledge that we "all fall short of the glory of God" and need a Savior (3:23).

Marriage brings enough challenges of its own every day—we don't also need God to oppose us. Rather, we need all the grace and favor we can get from Him and from our spouse.

What does a humble spouse look like? A humble spouse

- thinks of their spouse more than themselves and puts their needs first (Phil. 2:3–4).
- isn't afraid to admit when they're wrong and is willing to apologize and seek forgiveness.
- is teachable and seeks to learn from mistakes and failures.
- acknowledges that different doesn't necessarily mean right or wrong.
- isn't threatened by their spouse's wisdom, gifts, or passions.
- looks to Jesus as the greatest example of humility (vv. 5–11).

Humility looks good on everyone. It's one-size-fits-all, matches any outfit, and never goes out of style or season. Humility is one of the most attractive characteristics of any person, and this trait sets us up to be the spouse we want to be.

Heavenly Father, please help us to be humble. Help us to follow the perfect example of Your Son, Jesus Christ, who laid aside His rights and privileges to take our sins upon Himself and die in our place. While we know we don't have to die for the sins of our spouse, we know that we'll need to lay down our desires for their sake. Help us to think of our significant other before ourselves, and help us to follow the example of Jesus. We pray that our marriage will be marked by a Christlike humility.

DAY 31

Understanding

Husbands, in the same way be considerate as you live with your wives, and treat them with respect as the weaker partner and as heirs with you of the gracious gift of life, so that nothing will hinder your prayers.

1 Peter 3:7

One of my favorite verses in the whole Bible is today's verse for the character trait of understanding: 1 Peter 3:7. While this verse is addressed to husbands, the principle applies to both husbands and wives. Peter said we are to "be considerate" of our spouse. The English Standard Version translates this phrase as to live with each other "in an understanding way." The original Greek language takes it even further—we're to live with our spouse "according to knowledge." This means we need to do some work to understand more about our spouse.

Practically, what does it mean to live with your future spouse in an understanding way? Here are a few suggestions:

- *You take time to learn more about your spouse.* You ask them questions, and you listen to what they say. This starts when you date and get engaged and continues for all the days you have together as husband and wife. Don't make assumptions. Seek clarity and ask questions.
- *You're in tune with your spouse's ongoing needs.* You realize that these needs may change depending on how their day goes.
- *You pay attention to your spouse.* You honor them above yourself, as Romans 12:10 says: "Be devoted to one another in love. Honor one another above yourselves."
- *You pursue your spouse all the days you have together.* You go on dates, spend time together, and are attentive to their needs. My wife does this so well. She knows me intimately and can adjust how she cares for me based on my mood. When I have a bad day, she'll mourn with me. When it's a good day, she celebrates with me (v. 15).

Peter said if we don't pay attention to our spouse's needs, if we don't live with them according to knowledge, then our prayers may be hindered. There's a direct link between how you treat your spouse and how close you are with the Lord. God cares deeply about how you treat your spouse, and hopefully you do as well.

How are you and your significant other doing at seeking to understand each other? What can you do to understand each other more deeply, starting today?

God, we pray You'll help us take our eyes off ourselves and look at each other's needs. We pray that when we are married, we will live with each other according to knowledge in an understanding way, communicating that we care about each other. We confess we often care only about ourselves, so help us to care deeply about each other, knowing that how we love each other affects our relationship with You as well.

DAY 32

Teachable

Whoever loves discipline loves knowledge, but whoever hates correction is stupid.

Proverbs 12:1

My wife and I have four sons who are, at this moment of writing, ages eighteen, eighteen, fifteen, and thirteen. As you can imagine, there are plenty of opportunities for our family members to apologize to one another and seek and grant forgiveness. At times our sons argue and yell at each other. In other moments they tear each other down. In marriage, Kristen and I have had arguments and disagreements. We've even made each other cry on occasion.

Every time an argument breaks out in our family, we have an opportunity to learn and grow. We can either move forward with pride, thinking we're right and they're wrong, or we can choose to be teachable and learn from our sins and mistakes. Life constantly provides us with opportunities to learn. We'd all benefit from teachable spirits.

During your early years of marriage, you and your significant other will continue to get to know each other. You'll likely make assumptions based on your family of origin, and when your spouse doesn't do what you thought they'd do, you'll have the opportunity to choose how you respond. You're going to want to be very teachable so that you can grow in your marriage and so that you and your spouse can better understand how to love and serve each other.

A few years ago, I went to a marriage conference with about seventy-five other marriage ministry leaders. One of the speakers was Dr. Gary Chapman. If you've ever heard of *The 5 Love Languages*, then you've heard of Dr. Chapman. He's sold millions and millions of books. He's forgotten more about marriage than the rest of the world could ever know about it! Yet, at a marriage conference led and taught by much younger men and women, Dr. Chapman sat through every session and took notes. It was one of the greatest pictures of being teachable that I've ever seen.

What if we went into marriage with the same mentality? Our marriages would be much stronger if we stopped to listen, learn, and take notes. I pray you and your future spouse will be teachable in marriage.

Lord, we pray You'd help us be teachable. Help us be a husband and wife who are willing to learn. We pray that we'd never grow weary of loving knowledge and under-standing. Help us not to hate correction, as the writer of Proverbs 12 said. We pray we'd be humble, correctable, and teachable in our marriage.

DAY 33

Honest

The LORD detests lying lips, but he delights in people who are trustworthy.

Proverbs 12:22

I recently had a conversation with some friends about whether there are times it's permissible to lie. We collectively agreed it's okay to choose creatively what to share and what not to share while planning something like a surprise party or marriage proposal. Outside of that, I'd be hard-pressed to find occasions when it's okay for one person to lie to another.

Yet we live in a world where we consistently lie. We tell little white lies. We tell part of the truth but not the whole truth. Or maybe we exaggerate for the sake of a good story. We're not precise in our communication because we want others to be amazed by our adventures. Even though most of us have been told from a young age not to lie, it's easy to become careless with our words. The writer of Proverbs 12:22 said it so well. God detests our lying lips, but He delights in us when we're trustworthy. What will we choose to do as we communicate with others?

The challenge becomes even more pronounced in marriage. When you and your significant other pledge your lives to each other, you become one flesh (Gen. 2:24). Whatever you say or do impacts your spouse. So right now, even before you are married, it's time to leave behind the lazy, selfish habit of lies and instead be honest in your communication. The beauty of marriage is that you are to be naked without shame with your spouse (v. 25), meaning you should be able to share anything and everything with each other. The one-flesh relationship removes the excuse that you need to impress each other or exaggerate the truth.

This one may take some work for you in your marriage. Because many of us are used to telling lies, you may have some major shifts to make in how you communicate. For example, words like *always* and *never* probably don't belong in your marriage. ("I *always* take out the trash." "You *never* go shopping.") It may feel that way, but the truth is rarely *always* and *never*.

Most of us lied before we walked closely with Jesus. It's time to leave that behind. Paul wrote in Colossians 3:9, "Do not lie to each other, since you have taken off your old self with its practices." Leave your old self behind. Instead, be honest with each other as you honor God and your future spouse in your communication.

God, the pattern of the world tells us to lie, to say whatever we need to say to get ahead. We don't want to live this way. Instead, we want to honor You and each other with our honest lips. We don't want You working against us; rather, we want You to delight in us as we make trustworthy decisions. Help us to be honest with You, with each other, and with others.

DAY 34

Thoughtful

Do to others as you would have them do to you.

Luke 6:31

During the season that I was writing this book, I needed to make a difficult decision about my job. I have great peace about where I landed in the decision, but making it weighed heavily on me. At times I questioned my value on our church staff and battled insecurities about my ability to preach, lead others, and counsel couples. The decision I made will lead me to lose out on some relational time with some of my closest friends on staff. I'm feeling lonely even thinking of some of the relational challenges in my future since I will have less time with my friends. I've got a lot of Enneagram 4 in me, and I feel everything deeply.[1]

My wife, Kristen, is one of the most thoughtful people I've ever met. She's mindful of the needs of others and puts others before herself. She does to them as she would want them to do to her. She knows how to encourage others and is empathetic to the challenges they are facing.

Kristen knows me better than any person on this planet, so she knew I had some relational needs during this season. I'm writing this section about thoughtfulness on my forty-ninth birthday. Hard to believe, but by the time you're holding this book in your hands I'll be more than fifty years old! Anyway, I needed some encouragement on my birthday due to the challenges I mentioned earlier. In her thoughtfulness, Kristen made sure we had family dinner together. When we got home from dinner, she arranged to have some of my closest guy friends come over to hang out.

I hope you're a thoughtful person and are marrying someone who is also thoughtful. You want your spouse to be someone who thinks about you and is mindful of your needs (and vice versa). Those needs will be emotional, financial, physical, mental, and relational. A thoughtful spouse puts the needs of the other before their own (Phil. 2:3–4) and acts accordingly. To be thoughtful doesn't mean you simply think about others but act in such a way that you seek to help them in their needs.

Today, think of one small way you can serve your significant other. Let it be evidence of a selfless thoughtfulness.

God, we confess we tend to put our own needs and desires first and then think of our significant other if we have any margin left. Help us to turn this around and put the

*other's needs and desires first. We pray we'd be a husband
and wife who are thoughtful toward each other, consistently put the other first, and consider each other's needs
and act accordingly. Thank You for all the ways You are
thoughtful toward us.*

DAY 35

Celebratory

Be devoted to one another in love. Honor one another above yourselves.

Romans 12:10

Is your relationship marked by celebration? Do you enjoy celebrating your future spouse, or do you find yourself jealous of them at times? When I experience a win at work, home, in health, or in writing, Kristen is the first person I want to call or text. What sometimes can feel like gloating or boasting with others feels normal and right with your spouse.

As we have seen throughout this book, when you say "I do," you become one flesh with your spouse (Gen. 2:24). Their struggles become part of your struggles, and your wins become part of their victories. We bear each other's burdens as one and celebrate each other as one. One of the biggest blessings of marriage is having the ability and privilege of celebrating your spouse.

I thought about this idea of celebrating your spouse when I heard how a husband I know celebrated his wife's first day of work in a new position. She wasn't just starting a new job; she was starting a new career. He got her a new necklace, left a note for her in her purse, and gave her a special gift when she got home from work that afternoon.

Know how your significant other likes to celebrate. In *The 5 Love Languages*, Dr. Gary Chapman identified five primary ways people tend to show and receive love: words of affirmation, acts of service, quality time, physical touch, and receiving gifts.[1] The key to celebrating your spouse well is knowing their primary love language and demonstrating your love to them in that way.

Celebrate your spouse in a way that shows you know them and allows you to honor them above yourself. If they like celebrating their birthday, go big! Make it a birthday *week* instead of a birthday *day*. If they value quality time, set aside a weekend to celebrate your anniversary together. Find ways to celebrate the big moments of life as well as the small personal achievements.

What can you do, starting today, to make yours a relationship marked by celebration?

God, we pray we would be each other's biggest fans. Help us to celebrate each other well in a way that shows we know, value, and honor them above ourselves. Help us to put our preferences aside and put their desires above our own. We pray we would demonstrate our love for each other in how we celebrate each other every day.

DAY 36

Learning

And this is my prayer: that your love may abound more and more in knowledge and depth of insight.

Philippians 1:9

In my job as a marriage pastor, I have the privilege of helping couples grow and strengthen their marriages. In 2021, I started a class designed to enrich marriages through teaching, small group discussion, and homework. The first class was filled with couples ranging from newlyweds to a couple married for forty-four years. I'm encouraged by newlyweds who want to start their marriage right and more so by couples married for more than four decades who still want to improve their marriages. Couples who maintain a posture of learning will do well in marriage.

As you enter marriage, you may think you know just about everything about your significant other. But as followers of

Christ, ideally both you and your spouse will become more and more like Jesus Christ. I hope you will change for the better, and I hope your spouse will continue to change too. And as you both change, you will need to continue to be learners in marriage.

Kristen and I have been married since 2001. When we got married, I knew her main love language was quality time together. We enjoyed long dates, weekends of hanging out, and vacations, since these gave us such good one-on-one time. Fast-forward to 2004 when she gave birth to our twin sons, Duncan and Drew. Amid changing diapers, washing bottles, and soothing screaming babies, Kristen's love language quickly changed to acts of service. We were in a season where quality time together, while still important, wasn't her number one priority. Rather, the way I loved her best was by doing acts of service for her. I learned how to best serve and care for her during this unique season of our marriage.

In Philippians 1:9, Paul prays that our "love may abound" in "knowledge and depth of insight." He wasn't specifically praying for marriages, but the principles still apply. As you and your significant other gain knowledge and depth of insight into each other for a lifetime, may your love for each other abound more and more.

> God, help us to be lifelong learners about each other. Help us to be humble and teachable and willing to learn more and more about You and about each other. Help us also to be a husband and wife who desire to be known and who authentically live our lives as an open book with each other. We pray our increasing knowledge will allow our love to grow and our marriage to be strengthened.

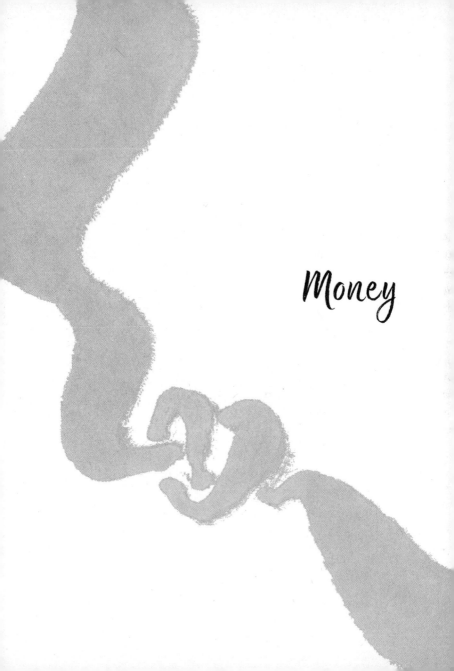

Money

DAY 37

Faithful Steward

Now it is required that those who have been given a trust must prove faithful.

1 Corinthians 4:2

It's too bad we don't use the word *stewardship* that often today. When someone stewards something well, it means they manage it well. The Lord has given every Christian gifts, resources, time, and money to manage, and we're accountable to the Lord for how we steward everything He's provided. Some people are given millions of dollars while others aren't given much cash, and some are given a great talent while others do not seem to have any outstanding abilities. Regardless, we're responsible for how we manage everything we have. As Paul said in 1 Corinthians 4:2, we're to prove ourselves faithful with all of it.

I'm thinking of three families who are stewards of a large sum of financial resources. They have beautiful homes and also incredible lake homes. What encourages me the most is how generous these families are with their lake homes. Various other families, church staffs, or ministries use these vacation homes weekly. These families have proven to be faithful with what God has entrusted to them.

What has God given to you and your spouse-to-be? What gifts and resources has He entrusted to you? In the future, you might have free time available to serve at your church or in the community. Or maybe you'll be like my friends and have a lake house you'll choose to open to others. Are you and your significant other aligned in your views on giving to your church? Have you discussed whether there are other like-minded nonprofit organizations you plan on giving money to?

One of the biggest challenges I see couples face is when one spouse is willing to be a good steward but the other isn't. This leads to conflict and resentment between husband and wife, and ultimately some couples aren't faithful with what the Lord has entrusted to them. Paul says it's *required* that those who have been entrusted with resources be faithful with them. It's not something God intends to be optional.

Are you and your future spouse on the same page about stewardship? This would be a good time to discuss it with each other. Take a few moments to pray that you and your significant other would be found faithful as you steward all God has given to you.

Lord, thank You for everything You've entrusted to us. You owe us nothing, yet You chose to give us resources, time, and gifts. Would You please help us to be faithful with them and help us to be aligned about how we manage everything? At times we'll want to be selfish, so we know we'll need Your help to be faithful, generous stewards of everything You entrust to us.

DAY 38

Thankful

Rejoice always, pray continually, give thanks in all circumstances; for this is God's will for you in Christ Jesus.

1 Thessalonians 5:16–18

What does it look like to have a marriage marked by thankfulness? When Paul wrote 1 Thessalonians 5:16–18, did he really mean that we're to give thanks in *all* circumstances? Did he really understand how hard life is and how challenging marriage can be at times? Did he really know how irritating *my* significant other can be on occasion? Why and how could I possibly give thanks for all of that?

Paul's life was marked by more trials than we can even comprehend. If you read Paul's words in 2 Corinthians 11:16–33, you'll see a list of some of the challenges he walked through.

If Paul could "give thanks in all circumstances," then you and I can do the same in our day-to-day relational challenges.

People whose lives are marked by thankfulness are a joy to be around. They acknowledge the kindness of others. They see when others serve them sacrificially and selflessly. And they take the time to tell others they appreciate them. Most of our lives are so marked by selfish navel-gazing that we don't take the time to thank others. Even more so, we miss out on opportunities to express gratitude to the Lord.

One area in which we often lack thankfulness is our money. We compare ourselves to others—cars, homes, clothes, salaries, and much more. What would it look like for you and your significant other to live with a mindset of gratitude for what the Lord has entrusted to you?

When we think and live rightly, we acknowledge the radical and sacrificial love of the Father, most clearly exemplified in the death of His Son, Jesus. I never want to get over that or used to it or think I deserve it in any way. When we grasp the work of the Father and Son, prompted in us by the Spirit, we become thankful people. And there's no better relationship in which to live this out every day than marriage.

One of the best practices I learned from others to help me become more thankful is to simply make a list, every morning, of three to five things I'm thankful for. This daily practice helps shift my heart away from focusing on myself to worshiping the Lord. Several times a week, something about my wife shows up on that gratitude list.

I highly recommend this daily discipline. As you close your time today, take out a pen or start a note on your phone and list five things you're grateful for about your significant other. Share your lists with each other. Now take a few moments to thank God for how He has made your significant other.

> *God, thank You for the way You have uniquely designed each of us. Thank You for bringing us together, and help us learn how to use our unique skills, gifts, and design to complement each other in our future marriage. We pray that You would help both of us become more like You as we seek to thank You and honor You in our relationship.*

DAY 39

Giving

He also saw a poor widow put in two very small copper coins. "Truly I tell you," he said, "this poor widow has put in more than all the others."

Luke 21:2–3

I distinctly remember the emotions I had when Kristen and I gave the largest amount of money we'd ever given at one time to our church in Dallas. It was a feeling of excitement and joy, knowing that we were giving to the mission of a church we believed in. Our church was raising money to buy property to build on instead of meeting weekly in a local high school.

At the same time I felt fear, because Kristen and I were giving away just about everything we had in savings. We knew we would need to depend on the Lord to provide, more than we ever had in our lives. I'm certain most people gave more money than we did, but the amount didn't matter—we were giving sacrificially.

In Luke 21, Jesus watched different people bringing financial gifts to the treasury. Most gave out of their wealth, but one poor widow gave out of her poverty. Jesus commended this widow for putting in more than all the others. Even though the amount was less, she gave to the treasury sacrificially.

It is important to be aligned with your significant other in your thoughts on money and giving. Now is the time to discuss if you're on the same page as your future spouse about giving to the Lord. Where will you give? Will you give to other ministries besides your church? How often will you give and how much? How will you decide when to give more?

It's convicting to me that the most Kristen and I ever gave was when we had almost nothing. We sacrificially gave to the Lord, and it's one of the highlights of my life. But as life has gotten busier and more complex with house bills, car insurance for our kids, and college tuition, I can find myself valuing our savings account more than sacrificial giving. Thankfully, Kristen and I have made it a priority to give more to our church and to other ministries, but it's still a challenge for us, as it is for most couples. Make sure you and your significant other are prayerfully aligned on your views of money and giving.

Lord, thank You for the amazing, faith-filled example of this poor widow from Luke 21. Thank You that Jesus took the time to highlight this woman's faith and to encourage her for her sacrificial giving. Help us to give sacrificially to our church and to ministries that do Your work in the world today. Keep us from putting more stock in our stuff and our savings than in giving to Your work.

DAY 40

Obedient

Whoever has my commands and keeps them is the one who loves me. The one who loves me will be loved by my Father, and I too will love them and show myself to them.

John 14:21

When I hear the word *obedient*, I think of children obeying their parents or a dog obeying its owner. Our family brought home our first dog in the middle of the pandemic, and we spent a fair amount of time trying to get our puppy to learn to obey. (We're over eighteen years in, and we're still working on our children!)

But obedience extends much further than children and pets. Every follower of Jesus Christ must learn what it means to obey the Lord. In John 14:21, Jesus said when we obey Him and keep His commandments, we demonstrate our love for Him.

If there's any area in which we especially need counsel on obedience, it's money. We tend to spend our resources on things we want, and in the process we can miss out on opportunities to give back to the Lord. At times, we can even love our stuff more than we love God. We get a unique opportunity to obey the Lord with our money.[1]

A lack of obedience to the Lord ought to lead us to question our love for Him. At a minimum, we display a lack of trust in Him when we disobey. When we disobey, it's as if we're telling God we trust ourselves more than we trust Him. If we fully trusted the Lord, we would fully obey Him, knowing His ways are greater than our sinful and selfish desires.

God's Word lays out His intentions and design for marriage, sexual intimacy, money, and so much more. Whenever we choose our own way, we are telling the Lord we know better—and we're not sure He knows what He's talking about. We doubt His goodness and question His love for us. For this reason, you'll want to pray that both you and your significant other are obedient to the Lord's commands, including commands about your money and giving. This doesn't always mean you'll get what you want, but a heart and posture of obedience communicate to the Lord that you trust Him and want to follow His ways for your life and marriage.

The actions we choose indicate what we believe. Choose to follow and obey the Lord, and obediently follow Him all the days He gives you breath. This demonstrates a faith that believes Him and pleases Him (Heb. 11:6) and demonstrates your love to and for the Lord (John 14:21).

> *Lord, help us to trust You in every part of our lives and future marriage. Out of this trust, we want to choose to obey You all the days of our lives, including the area of our finances. Thank You for Your design of marriage, and we pray we will follow You so that it would go well for us in life and in marriage. Thank You for being worthy of our full obedience and trust.*

DAY 41

Hospitable

Rather, he must be hospitable, one who loves what is good, who is self-controlled, upright, holy and disciplined.

Titus 1:8

During our twenty-two years of marriage, Kristen and I have been shown incredible hospitality by some married couples. I think of one couple who always has our favorite drinks on hand when we come over for dinner. I think of another friend who gives gifts to guests who visit their home. Other families generously share their lake homes and show great hospitality to anyone who uses these homes. These families seem to come alive when they invite others over for meals and conversation.

In Titus 1:5–9, Paul laid out qualifications for church elders. He detailed some required character qualities of an elder, including self-control, uprightness, holiness, and discipline. Paul also said an elder must be hospitable (v. 8). This means they must be willing to be generous and welcoming to guests and visitors. The fact that the Holy Spirit inspired Paul to pen these words indicates the importance to God of being hospitable and welcoming.

A hospitable couple places a priority on stewarding what God has entrusted to them in their home. They invite fellow followers of Christ over for meals. They play games and enjoy one another's company. They also invite nonbelievers into their home. They share their lives, and they share the gospel with people who need to know Jesus.

Kristen and I moved to Waco, Texas, in the summer of 2020. One of our favorite things about Waco is that it's a college town, and we get to engage with Baylor University students from all over the country. Every semester we open up our home and invite students over for games, food, and a home away from their hometown. We love getting to be hospitable together as a couple by inviting students to our house.

Maybe as newlyweds you won't own a home or even have the money to make meals for others. But you can always invite others over for dessert and a game night, no matter where you live. Being a hospitable couple has nothing to do with how much money you make, how fancy your home is, or how well you can cook. Rather, it's a heart disposition that wants to share your lives with others. You see your marriage as an opportunity to invite others over for fellowship.

Discuss with your significant other how you plan on being hospitable as newlyweds. What are some ways you can show hospitality to friends and neighbors?

God, we pray we would be a hospitable couple. Help us to see our home as a place to encourage and love others. We want to be good stewards of everything You've entrusted to us, including our home. We pray that we would be hospitable, warm, kind, and inviting, and that we'd see our home as a place to share the gospel with nonbelievers and to encourage and teach believers.

DAY 42

Determined

To this end I strenuously contend with all the energy Christ so
powerfully works in me.

Colossians 1:29

There's a lot we can learn from the apostle Paul's words to the
church in Colossae. Even though he never met the Colossians
in person, he was determined to do all he could to help them
grow and mature in Christ. He was writing to them while in
chains (4:18). Don't just rush by that. While imprisoned, he
was writing to a group of people he'd never met, and he was
striving and contending for them to grow in their relationship
with Christ. How different would your life and relationship
look if you strenuously contended for your relationship with
Christ and your significant other as Paul did for the Colossians?

143

I've been ministering to couples almost every day since 2006, and I've seen too many lazy spouses. They're determined to finish the next season of their favorite show on Netflix. They're determined to keep up with friends on social media. They're determined to make viral TikTok videos. But they're not determined to work hard for their family or marriage. I've watched one spouse work hard while the other stays at home, unemployed and spending time and energy on video games. They're determined to excel as an unpaid gamer, but they are not determined to provide for their family or fight for their marriage. (Of course, I am not talking about most stay-at-home parents, who work just as hard or even harder than a spouse who holds a paying job.)

In addition to praying for determination in your marriage, I'd like to suggest that you and your significant other have a conversation about how hard you're willing to work for your marriage and for your household. Pray together that you will faithfully work hard for your family, whether you are working to provide income for your household or working at home to raise your children. Paul later wrote in Colossians 3:23, "Whatever you do, work at it with all your heart, as working for the Lord, not for human masters." He also wrote in 1 Corinthians 10:31, "So whether you eat or drink or whatever you do, do it all for the glory of God."

When someone is determined, it means they're firmly resolved in their efforts. They have a direction they want to go, and they strive to get there. They discuss dreams and goals for their family and take action to make these desires come true. For example, you may decide you want to travel to the beach together as a family every summer. A couple who is determined to make this desire a reality must be aligned on how they're going to make it happen. Make sure you and your significant other are resolved to strenuously contend together.

God, we pray we would be determined to contend for our relationship with You and with each other. Help us to work hard to provide and care for our household and to be determined to work with excellence and for Your glory in all we do. Help us not to be lazy but to work with all our hearts, as though we're working for You.

DAY 43

Content

I am not saying this because I am in need, for I have learned to
be content whatever the circumstances. I know what it is to be
in need, and I know what it is to have plenty. I have learned the
secret of being content in any and every situation, whether well
fed or hungry, whether living in plenty or in want.

Philippians 4:11–12

One of the challenges you'll face in marriage is the temptation
to compare your marriage to the marriages of others. You'll
see the highlights on social media, in the workplace, at family
gatherings, at church, and much more. When you see someone's
highlights and compare them to the reality of your marriage,
you may feel discontent. What you see may make it appear that
your marriage isn't good enough. You could also believe you
need more money, better kids, or a nicer home. You might lack
contentment in any and every situation.

We have much to learn from the apostle Paul. In Philippians 4:11–12, Paul said he learned "the secret of being content," whether in plenty or in need. Even though he faced persecution and beatings, Paul somehow stayed content in all circumstances. What if we did the same? What if no matter what challenges we face, we stayed content?

This is an area in which you and your spouse will need to pray for and help each other. Choose to be a spouse who remains content, and pray your spouse would be the same. It's easy to look around and compare. I've heard it said that instead of coveting your neighbor's green grass, stop looking over the fence at their yard and instead water your own lawn. In other words, quit looking around and comparing your relationship to others', and instead work on your own relationship.

Do the hard work it requires to have a thriving marriage, have a whole lot of fun along the way, and choose to be content in any and every situation. The way not to struggle with a lack of contentment is to work on your own relationship and to live with a constant attitude of gratitude.

> *Lord, we pray You would always be enough for us. When we are tempted to look around and compare our lives to what we see on social media or in others' lives, remind us that You are all we need. Help us not to compare our relationship with others'. Help us to know and live out the secret Paul discussed in Philippians 4:11–12 so that we would be a contented couple.*

DAY 44

Generous

Remember this: Whoever sows sparingly will also reap sparingly, and whoever sows generously will also reap generously. Each of you should give what you have decided in your heart to give, not reluctantly or under compulsion, for God loves a cheerful giver.

2 Corinthians 9:6–7

In 2 Corinthians 9:6–7, Paul encouraged the believers in the church of Corinth to be generous with their possessions and in their giving. God desires for His people to be cheerful givers, not to give out of compulsion or because we have to. God wants His children to be givers, not takers, and He wants us to experience the joy and blessing of generosity.

Most of us love our birthdays. We eat cake, get gifts, and receive texts, DMs, and emails with birthday greetings. When it's your birthday, it's all about you. Unless you're my friend, boss, and pastor, Jonathan "JP" Pokluda. On his birthday, he turns it around and uses it as an opportunity to give to others. Instead of getting gifts on his birthday, he often gives gifts to others. He takes the focus off himself and makes his birthday an opportunity to exercise his gift of generosity.

What if you and your significant other learned from this example and modeled generosity toward each other? Instead of taking and waiting to be served, what if you turned it around and chose to be generous every day to your future spouse?

Consider some of the ways you and your spouse can be generous with each other after you are married:

- What if you are generous in your encouragement of your spouse, and you look for opportunities to encourage and affirm them?
- What if you generously serve your spouse by taking on tasks around the house that you know they dislike?
- What if, after you are married, you choose to be a generous lover in the bedroom, and you put their needs and desires before your own?
- What if you choose to be generous in giving to your church? You can view your possessions and resources as an opportunity to be a blessing to others.

We live in a me-centered, selfish world. God wants us to be generous to each other and to others. Let's pray that we would follow His Word, not the world.

God, You modeled perfectly for us what it looks like to be generous. You gave Your one and only Son for us, to die for our sins. Help us in our marriage, when we feel selfish and don't want to serve each other, to look to You and follow Your lead. We pray our marriage and our lives would be marked by a Christlike generosity in all we do.

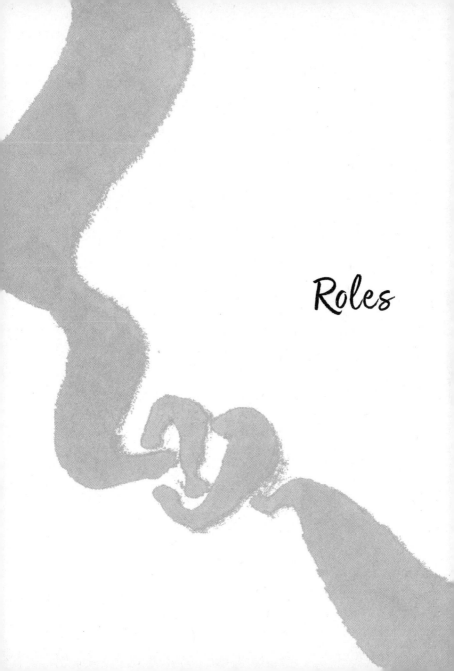

Roles

DAY 45

Submissive to God

> Submit yourselves, then, to God. Resist the devil, and he will flee from you.
>
> James 4:7

Most people don't like the word *submission*. They think it's an outdated term meant to imply women are inferior to men. But biblically, there isn't a hint that women are inferior (Gal. 3:28). This word has been hijacked to have a negative connotation. In the Bible, *submission* is a Christlike term. We see Jesus the Son submit to the will of God the Father (John 6:38). This doesn't mean the Father is greater than the Son, but the Son does willingly submit to God the Father.

In James 4:7, the apostle James told believers to submit ourselves to God. Coupled with this command is another instruction to resist the devil so that he will flee from us. We know a few things about Satan. We know he prowls around like a roaring lion looking to devour us (1 Pet. 5:8). We know Satan is the father of lies, and there is no truth in him (John 8:44).

A Christian marriage will face attacks from the world and from the enemy, so we need to do all we can to fight back against the evil schemes of the enemy. Satan would love to tear down your marriage, and he would like for your marriage to fail, like many others. He wants Christian marriages to look just like the marriages of the world. If the two of you want a standing chance in your marriage, then you must submit your lives to God's leadership.

It seems like we're surrounded by divorce. Perhaps your parents are divorced, or some close friends have gone through a divorce. Maybe divorce is even part of your own story. Marriage takes hard work and requires two people willing to work on the relationship. When a couple submits to the Lord, prays together on a consistent basis, and remains active in a local, healthy church, then their odds of getting a divorce plummet.

I want your marriage to thrive. The most important step you can take is to submit everything you have in your life and marriage to God's authority. If you're dating or are engaged to someone who's not willing to submit themselves to God, then I would take immediate steps either to end or drastically change your relationship.

I have so much hope for your relationship. I've seen many couples thrive when they willingly submit their lives and their marriage to the Lord.

God, we admit it's hard to submit to You at times. Help us to each submit our life to You. We need all the help we can get against the evil schemes of the devil, so we beg You to help us to submit to You and to resist the enemy. Help us embrace the roles You've given us in marriage and in relationship with You.

DAY 46

Respectful

However, each one of you also must love his wife as he loves himself, and the wife must respect her husband.

Ephesians 5:33

At the end of the longest passage about marriage in the Bible, the apostle Paul said the husband must love his wife and the wife must respect her husband. The husband should also respect his wife, and the wife should seek to love her husband. We often talk about love when it comes to marriage, but we don't often talk about what it means to be respectful.

In his commentary on Ephesians, Dr. Tom Constable described love and respect in marriage like this: "If the husband loves his wife the way Christ demonstrated His love for the church, the wife will naturally respect and consequently love her husband."[1] When a husband does his job of leading and loving his wife well, he makes her job of respecting him much easier. A husband can look for ways every day to love and serve his wife selflessly and sacrificially. This can be as small as washing the dishes or as big as taking her on her dream vacation for an anniversary. And this also applies to wives—a wife who loves her husband well makes it easy for him to respect her.

Many people I know, present company included, struggle in how we view ourselves. While we may present like we've got it together, beneath the surface many of us struggle with insecurity and negative self-talk. In marriage, we have a unique opportunity to help our significant other reject the lies and believe what's true.

What are some ways you can be respectful of your future spouse?

- *Ask them how they're doing.* Ask them to share the highs and lows of their day. Pray for them about their job and don't belittle or mock them.
- *Encourage them.* When they pursue you, affirm them for their desire to love you well. When they engage well with the children, tell them what a great parent they are.
- *Learn to speak their love language.* Dr. Gary Chapman identified five common "love languages"—words of affirmation, quality time, physical touch, acts of service, and receiving gifts.[2] (If you don't know each other's love language, take the quiz at 5lovelanguages.com.[3]) For example, if your spouse responds to words of affirmation, then write them an encouraging note. If they value quality

time, then plan a date where you can spend a full day together.

Do you respect your future spouse? Does your future spouse show respect to you? Thank and encourage them for the ways they do this well.

Lord, help us to show respect to each other in marriage. Help us to consider the other more important than ourselves. We pray our marriage will be marked by respect. Help us to love each other well and to show respect to one another. Will You please show us ways we can better encourage one another in every facet of life?

DAY 47

Courageous

Have I not commanded you? Be strong and courageous. Do not be afraid; do not be discouraged, for the LORD your God will be with you wherever you go.

Joshua 1:9

Take a good look around you, and you'll see a lot of mess in the world: mass shootings, poverty, sickness and disease, and broken families. I spend most of my days counseling broken families and others who are struggling to keep theirs from breaking in the first place. So many men and women get married, struggle, and then give up in the midst of adversity and challenge.

It takes courage to make it as a married couple today. Even choosing to get married takes courage. Thriving marriages break the mold of what we often see around us. And this is what I hope and pray for you: that you would be strong and courageous and fight for your marriage so that your relationship is not like many of the marriages around you.

When we're bold and courageous, we take a stand. We fight for things that matter. We do what we need to do and say what we need to say. When the world tells us it's okay to give up, we keep fighting for our marriages and families.

What does courage look like in a Christian marriage?

- *Courage means you're willing to have hard conversations with your spouse*. Instead of sweeping issues under the rug or choosing to yell at each other, you make the decision to discuss challenges. It takes courage to listen and to ask good questions.

- *Courage means expressing your needs and desires*. Instead of suppressing your needs, you share them with your spouse.

- *Courage means you decide together to give to your church*. You are obedient and generous, even when finances are tight.

- *Courage means you trust God when things are tough*. You choose to keep trusting the Lord, no matter what comes your way.

Be courageous and do not be afraid. And do you know why you can be courageous? Joshua 1:9 says, "The LORD your God will be with you wherever you go." You can be courageous because you are never on your own.

Lord, sometimes it seems easier to quit or appease others. Help us to be strong and courageous, and help us to fight for the things that matter. Our marriage matters, so please help us to be bold and courageous. Help us to have the hard conversations, to make our marriage a priority, and to trust that You are with us wherever we go.

DAY 48

Strong

Blessed are those whose strength is in you.

Psalm 84:5

I have a love/hate relationship with the gym. I love walking on a treadmill while reading books on my Kindle. It's one of the highlights of my day. On the other hand, I hate strength training. I don't like lifting weights or using any kind of weight machine. While I am a big guy, no one would confuse me for someone physically strong. Per pound of body weight, I'm probably one of the weakest guys in the state of Texas.

The best Christian marriages are made of two strong people. If this sentence referred to physical strength, then my marriage would be in deep trouble. Fortunately, I'm talking about something much more significant than physical strength. A healthy marriage requires two people who find their strength in the Lord.

The writer of Psalm 84 said we are blessed when we find our strength in the Lord. As followers of Christ, we don't find our strength in our bench press max, our résumé, our bank account, or our social media following. The ones who are truly strong find their strength in the Lord. This is an overhaul for most of us, since we typically look for our strength in our achievements and our stuff, not in our relationship with Jesus.

How can you become strong in the Lord?

- *Read God's Word.* A friend once told me the key to consistently reading God's Word is to have a plan, place, and time for it. Know in advance *what* you're going to read in the Word, *where* you're going to read it, and what *time* you're going to do so.
- *Pray.* Every day you read a devotion from this book and pray to the Lord, you're strengthening your relationship with the Lord and your relationship with your significant other.
- *Invite others in.* Allow others to strengthen you through encouragement and sharpening words (Prov. 27:17).
- *Confess your sins to God and others.* When you confess your sins, you find healing, which leads to strength (James 5:16).

In Ecclesiastes 4:12, Solomon said, "Though one may be overpowered, two can defend themselves. A cord of three strands is not quickly broken." A husband and wife who walk with the Lord become a cord of three strands. And as Solomon said, this type of marriage is not easily broken. May you and your spouse form an unbreakable cord when you both find your strength in the Lord.

> *God, we need You to strengthen our relationships both with You and with each other. We know the world does all it can to weaken our faith, and the enemy would love nothing more than to tear a Christian marriage apart. That's why we need You to make us stronger every day. May our cord of three strands in marriage not be easily broken.*

DAY 49

Diligent

The lazy do not roast any game, but the diligent feed on the riches of the hunt.

Proverbs 12:27

All significant relationships require being diligent. Rarely can we attain something significant or healthy in life without much effort. This certainly holds true for marriage. If you want the marriage God intends for you to have and the marriage you've dreamed of and hoped for, then you must be diligent.

When Kristen and I sat down with Debbie for our premarital counseling, we thought we had a near-perfect relationship. It didn't matter what our premarital survey said or what Debbie told us, we were convinced that we wouldn't need to work hard on our marriage. After all, we loved each other, and we had worked through some challenges the first time we dated—what could possibly go wrong?

Though we've had a fairly smooth road in marriage so far, Kristen and I have had to work hard to thrive as a married couple. Strong marriages take effort.

Proverbs 12:27 tells us that if we're lazy, we will "not roast any game," meaning we won't exhibit Christ-honoring behaviors and communication in our marriage. We'll struggle, and at best we'll survive. But if we're diligent, we'll "feed on the riches of the hunt." This means we'll honor God and enjoy each other in marriage, no matter what circumstances we face. If we're diligent, we'll be prepared for any challenge before us.

Solomon said in Ecclesiastes 9:10, "Whatever your hand finds to do, do it with all your might." Marriage is the most significant human relationship you'll ever have, so it will be worth your effort to work at it "with all your might."

What does it look like to be diligent in marriage?

- You'll always be a student of your spouse (1 Pet. 3:7).
- You'll work hard at pursuing peace and unity (Rom. 12:18; Eph. 4:3).
- You'll serve your spouse instead of waiting to be served (Mark 10:45).
- You'll actively seek ways to have fun with each other (Eccles. 9:9).

Are you and your future spouse diligent in the ways listed above? Take a moment to encourage your significant other for one specific way they conscientiously work on your relationship.

God, help us to work hard on our marriage. Please help us to be diligent in every part of our lives together as husband and wife. Help us learn early in our marriage that it's worthwhile to serve our spouse with love. We pray we'd be diligent in every part of our marriage, so we would "feed on the riches of the hunt." God, please help us to put in the effort even when we don't believe it's worth it. Thank You, Jesus, for modeling a diligent life in all You did.

DAY 50

Appreciative

He who finds a wife finds what is good and receives favor from the LORD.

Proverbs 18:22

A few weeks ago, my family stayed at a friend's lake house during our kids' spring break. With four sons, you can imagine how much food we consume as a family! My wife worked and planned to make sure we had enough food for our four days there, which included multiple trips to several grocery stores to ensure we had everything. She also brought food and supplies for our double doodle dog, Bauer, and enough games to keep us entertained. She made sure we all packed everything we'd need for our getaway.

I'm always appreciative of my wife, but on trips like this, I'm especially so. I'm grateful for her planning, her attention to details, and her willingness to serve our family so well. As the writer of Proverbs 18:22 said, I've found "what is good."

This verse applies to both husbands and wives. When you find your spouse, you find what's good and receive favor from the Lord. While you may frustrate each other and drive each other crazy at times, your spouse is a gift from the Lord. It's easy to focus on your differences and the traits that annoy you. As you work through your differences and frustrations, I'd encourage you to appreciate deeply the gift your spouse is to you.

Celebrate the ways your spouse-to-be makes you better. Look for ways to celebrate their gifts and personality. Keep your eyes open for the things they're incredible at that can strengthen your marriage and your relationship with Christ.

What can you do today to show your appreciation?

Thank You, Lord, for the gift we are to each other. Thank You for how You made us, for the gifts we each have, and for the ways we make each other better. We pray we would always appreciate each other, and we ultimately appreciate You as the giver of good gifts. As James said, "Every good and perfect gift is from above, coming down from the Father of the heavenly lights, who does not change like shifting shadows" (1:17). Thank You for the gift of marriage, and thank You for helping us find what is good.

DAY 51

Dependable

His master replied, "Well done, good and faithful servant! You have been faithful with a few things; I will put you in charge of many things. Come and share your master's happiness!"

Matthew 25:23

Followers of Christ don't always do the best job of setting ourselves apart from a lost and messed-up world. Our actions and attitudes often look the same as everyone else's, and our marriages don't look that different either.[1] Christians have a reputation for being hypocritical, judgmental, and closed-minded. As you move toward marriage, you have an opportunity to distinguish yourselves from such negative attitudes about Christians.

You may not know this yet, but the Lord holds you responsible for how you live as a husband or wife. He has given you the gift of marriage, and I want to see you thrive in this gift. The world takes notice when it sees a healthy marriage, because healthy marriages stick out from the more difficult ones all around us. Marriage is the best picture we have of God's love for us, so it is not a relationship any one of us should take lightly.

In Matthew 25:14–30, Jesus told a parable about three individuals who were each entrusted with some possessions. Two handled the responsibility well and were dependable, but the third squandered the opportunity and broke trust with the master. The dependable servants heard, "Well done, good and faithful servant" from their master (vv. 21, 23).

I want you to hear God say, "Well done, good and faithful servant" about your marriage, as you likewise prove yourselves dependable in how you steward the gift of marriage. When we're dependable, it means we're reliable and worthy of trust. Here are a few questions to help you evaluate the dependability of you and your significant other:

- Are you dependable in your job? Do you do what you say you're going to do? Would your boss describe you as a dependable employee?
- Are you dependable in your interactions with each other? Do you keep your commitments, or do you break promises to your significant other?
- Would your parents and closest friends describe each of you as dependable?

If the answer to any of these questions is no, I'd caution you about moving forward in your relationship. You and your future spouse are going to spend decades together in marriage, Lord willing, and you don't want to be in a covenant relationship with someone who takes their responsibilities lightly. I'm cheering you on that you would hear, "Well done, good and faithful servant."

> *God, we pray You would help us to be dependable in our relationships with You and others. We pray that we will keep our word and strive to hear, "Well done, good and faithful servants" as good stewards of our marriage, for our good and Your glory. We need You to help us be people who stick to our commitments.*

DAY 52

Sacrificial

Follow God's example, therefore, as dearly loved children and walk in the way of love, just as Christ loved us and gave himself up for us as a fragrant offering and sacrifice to God.

Ephesians 5:1–2

It's incredible to think of what Jesus did on the cross for us. In fact, *incredible* falls far short when you consider that the perfect Son of God died for sinners like you and me. He gave Himself up that we may have life. In turn, we are to follow His example in the way we live. Paul said we are to "walk in the way of love, just as Christ loved us" (Eph. 5:2).

As He often does, Jesus turns our world upside down and breaks our paradigms. The world trains us to put ourselves first, while Christ's sacrificial love exemplifies putting others first. To live sacrificially is a huge challenge and comes at a high personal cost. To be sacrificial, we need to have a selfless love for others. We must learn to put the needs and desires of our spouse before our own.

My wife does this so well. I have watched Kristen sacrificially love me and our kids in countless ways. Every night during the school year, she puts aside her needs and desires so that she can serve our kids sacrificially by making sure they have lunches made, homework completed, and schoolbags packed. She engages our kids every night with heart questions and prays for them before she goes to sleep. At any given time, she has a massive to-do list, but she still manages to put the needs of others first.

If you want a great marriage, you and your future spouse should look no further than the example of Jesus. The best way to prepare well for marriage is by studying more about Him and then choosing to become more like Him. That's better advice than you'll find in any marriage book, podcast, or sermon. Follow God's example, and even though things won't always get easier, God can still use anything or anyone to help us grow.

Lord, thank You for perfectly modeling what sacrificial love looks like. We confess it's difficult to put the needs of others first, especially the needs of our partner. It should be easy, but sometimes serving our spouse will be more challenging than any other human relationship. As Paul challenged us to do in Ephesians 5:1–2, help us follow Your example and walk in the way of love.

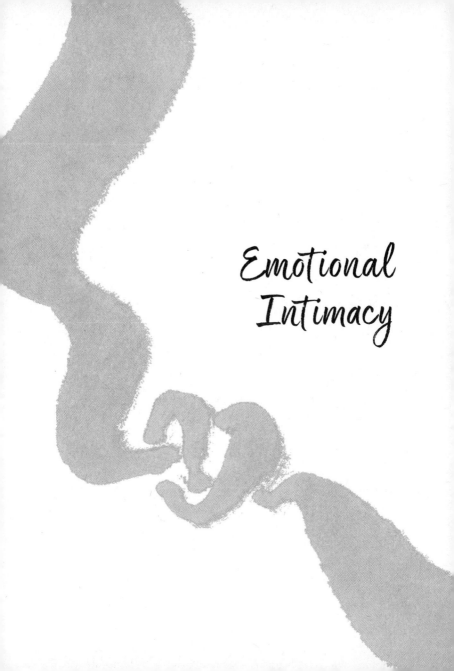

Emotional
Intimacy

DAY 53

Authentic

If we claim to have fellowship with him and yet walk in the darkness, we lie and do not live out the truth. But if we walk in the light, as he is in the light, we have fellowship with one another, and the blood of Jesus, his Son, purifies us from all sin.

1 John 1:6–7

When we say someone is authentic, we mean they're real or genuine—they're not counterfeit or fake. An authentic $100 bill is worth $100. A counterfeit bill is worthless. The same holds true in marriage—an inauthentic spouse or marriage lacks value. But a real, authentic marriage is priceless.

We live in a world marked by inauthenticity that celebrates appearances—Instagram highlight reels, putting our best foot forward, and hiding our mistakes and sins. Even churches are filled with people who put on their Sunday best. Yet we long to be free and real. We want to be fully known and fully loved. But until we're fully authentic, we can never be fully loved. The apostle John challenged us to "walk in the light, as [Jesus] is in the light" (1 John 1:7). When we do so, we can have fellowship with others and intimacy with Christ through His shed blood.

Before I proposed to Kristen, I wanted her to know all my secrets. I wanted to live in the light with her, and I shared my past sins, my current struggles, and my future hopes and dreams. I didn't want to feel like I was hiding the ugly parts of my life. God designed us to be naked without shame with our spouse in marriage (Gen. 2:25); when we are, we can be fully known and fully loved. I have watched secrets destroy lives and marriages.

I'm praying for you as I type these words, that you and your significant other would be authentic with each other. I want you both to be fully known and fully loved. The beauty of it all is that Jesus already knows everything about you, and He still chooses to love you. You are fully known by Him and fully loved by Him. I pray the same is true of your marriage in the way you see each other.

> *God, we confess that we want others to be impressed by us. We want them to see the good, and we want to hide the bad. Lord, we pray that we will be people who don't fear being real. Help us to be authentic with ourselves and with each other. Help us to deal with the fears and insecurities that come with being authentic. Thank You for knowing us fully and still loving us. Help us to do the same for each other.*

DAY 54

Compassionate

When he saw the crowds, he had compassion on them, because
they were harassed and helpless, like sheep without a shepherd.

Matthew 9:36

In John 11, Jesus wept at the death of His friend Lazarus. In
Matthew 15, at the feeding of the four thousand, Jesus had
compassion for the people because He cared about their health.
In Luke 7, Jesus felt compassion for a mother who had lost her
son. We are very fortunate to have many examples in the Bible
describing the compassion of Jesus Christ. And since we're to
become more and more like Jesus, we know we can continue
to grow in compassion toward others, especially toward our
future spouse.

What would it look like for your upcoming marriage to be marked by compassion? What if, when you saw your spouse struggling, you entered into their struggle and walked beside them through it? Marriages often look like the reverse, where instead of being on the same team, couples seem opposed to each other. Most people are not naturally compassionate—we need to ask God to help us grow in Christlike compassion.

What does it mean to be compassionate? It means when someone struggles, you struggle with them. You help bear their burdens and seek to carry their struggles with them. At its core it means to suffer with someone else. In marriage, since you're one flesh with your spouse (Gen. 2:24), their struggles become yours and your struggles become theirs.

Marriage seems to be the most likely relationship in which to be compassionate with another human being. But even married couples often miss out on compassion because we tend to be selfish and know showing compassion toward our spouse will cost us time. Furthermore, we know that showing compassion means taking on the other person's burdens and challenges, and we often don't want to make this effort. Also, some people struggle with accessing their emotions, making it more challenging to relate to the emotions of another human being.

But Jesus, being both fully God and fully man, was able to relate to the challenges of others. He deeply cared for and suffered with others. This was fully manifested when He took our sins and struggles upon Himself. Jesus's death on the cross is the ultimate expression of compassion. We get the privilege of following in His footsteps as we show compassion to others, especially toward our spouse.

Lord Jesus, thank You for demonstrating compassion to Your people. You took on our problems and challenges to the point of death on the cross. Thank You for modeling what it looks like to be compassionate. We pray You'll help us to do the same for each other. We need Your help to show compassion in our marriage.

DAY 55

Merciful

But God, being rich in mercy, because of the great love with which he loved us, even when we were dead in our trespasses, made us alive together with Christ—by grace you have been saved.

Ephesians 2:4–5 ESV

Many years ago, I heard someone define *mercy* as "not getting what you deserve." For example, let's suppose that one of my children plays football in my house and breaks a window. If I buy a new window and pay someone to replace it (thus sparing my child the financial cost), I am showing that child mercy since I'm paying the price for them, instead of making them pay for the repair. Likewise, God, who is "rich in mercy" (Eph. 2:4), doesn't give us the punishment we deserve if we trust in Jesus for the forgiveness of our sins. Instead of you and I paying the price for our sins, Jesus took the punishment for us—sparing us from eternal punishment and separation from Himself—through His mercy toward us. The price has been paid by Jesus, and God doesn't give us what we deserve.

Your marriage will be filled with opportunities for you to show mercy to your spouse. You'll both do things you said you wouldn't do, and won't do things you said you would do. You'll forget to empty the dishwasher, you'll use up the last roll of toilet paper and forget to replace it, or you'll accidentally leave one of your kids at a baseball game. (Please don't judge me—he was eleven, was hanging with his friends, and I thought Kristen had him. I went back and got him after five minutes!)

When we're merciful to each other in marriage, we create a safe place for deeper emotional intimacy with each other. We can know each other and be known by the other without fearing rejection.

In the same way the Lord shows mercy to us, we are to show mercy to our spouse. If the perfect God of the universe can spare you and me of what we rightfully deserve, then certainly we can do the same for each other. Our natural inclination typically leans toward justice and revenge—we want others to get what they deserve. This plays out even with our spouse, the one we love until death parts us. We want others to extend mercy to us, but we struggle to extend this same mercy to others.

The next time your significant other messes up, let your first step be showing mercy.[1] Remember God showed you mercy and try to do the same toward your spouse. When you show mercy, you'll carry less of a weight around with you, and your spouse will likely extend mercy back your way when you are the one falling short.

> *God, we're terrified to think of what we deserve because of our sins. We know we deserve punishment and separation from You, but You are rich in mercy. Your Son, Jesus, took the punishment we deserve for our sins, and we're eternally grateful for Your mercy. Please help us to extend this same mercy toward each other. Thank You, Lord.*

DAY 56

Happy

Taste and see that the LORD is good; blessed is the one who takes refuge in him.

Psalm 34:8

When my family moved from Dallas to Waco in the summer of 2020, my wife made a promise to our four sons. She told them that since it would be a big challenge moving in the middle of high school and middle school, while we were all living through a pandemic, we would get a family dog. They'd been asking for a dog for years, and we finally caved and brought home our family's first dog, a double doodle named Bauer.

As you can imagine, this made our boys happy to no end. Bauer is the most fun dog—he loves people, he's playful, and he enjoys being around us. He's made all six of us happy, and he's been the perfect addition to our family. At the same time, we all know Bauer can never become the ultimate source of our happiness. He eats socks, throws up on the carpet, and barks all night long when we take him on vacation. Someday in the future he'll die. As much as we love Bauer, we cannot make him the main reason we're happy.

While I love my dog, that doesn't even remotely compare to the way I feel about my wife. I love her with a completely different type of love. She brings me great joy, I love spending time with her, and she makes me happy, often just by walking into the room. Of course, she's human, so she inevitably will let me down, disappoint me, and likewise cannot be the primary source of my happiness. The same applies to the way she feels about me.

As you get ready to tie the knot, find someone who finds their happiness primarily in the Lord. As David said in Psalm 34:8, "Blessed is the one who takes refuge in him." The word *blessed* in this verse can best be translated as "happy." In fact, many times when we see the word *blessed* in the Bible, it's best translated as "happy" (see Matt. 5:3–11). We are to find our happiness in the Lord—let your source be Him, not your spouse.

At the same time, I hope you and your future spouse realize your blessings, which in turn will make you happy. Spending "till death do us part" with an unhappy person can make your time on earth feel like an eternity. Find your happiness in the Lord, and it will affect your happiness as you live life as a married couple.

Lord, we confess that we can seek after so many things in this world that make us temporarily happy. We find happiness in stuff and settle for less way too easily. Help us to find our joy and our true happiness in You—and in You alone. Help us not to expect our spouse to be the source of our happiness. May we release the pressure from ourselves to make each other feel happy.

DAY 57

Empathetic

Rejoice with those who rejoice; mourn with those who mourn.

Romans 12:15

A few years ago, when I turned forty-four, I joined my nine-year-old and thirteen-year-old in getting braces on my teeth. Before I got them, to my shame, I'd never asked my sons any questions about their braces. I didn't ask about the colored bands around their brackets, I didn't ask what they could or couldn't eat, and I didn't ask if they had any pain after getting their teeth worked on. But as soon as I got my braces, I had a million questions for them! Suddenly, I cared what it was like to be them. Once I walked in their shoes (put on their teeth?), I developed empathy for them.

Empathy can be defined as the ability to understand and share the feelings of another. In marriage, it means we connect with our spouse because we understand their joys and pains. We see things from their perspective and think beyond ourselves. We live with them "in an understanding way" (1 Pet. 3:7 ESV).

Many couples lack empathy in their marriage. They see things from their own perspective only, without acknowledging what their spouse might be going through or feeling. This view is myopic and selfish, and works against God's design of a husband and wife being one flesh (Gen. 2:24).

The couple whose marriage is marked by empathy rejoices with their spouse when they're joyful and mourns with them when they're sad. They serve their spouse by connecting with them in a way that says they see, know, and care for them.

Here are a few ways you can grow in empathy with your spouse:

- *Be curious*. Ask them open-ended questions.
- *Be observant*. They're wired differently than you are, so make efforts to see from their point of view.
- *Listen to them*. Hint: when they communicate with you, put your phone away.
- *Pray*. Ask the Lord to help you to be more empathetic in your marriage.
- *Spend time together*. Never underestimate the benefit of quality time together and the ministry of presence.

Look for one way today you can show empathy to your future spouse. Ask them questions about their day and envision yourself "walking in their shoes" so you better understand their highs and lows of today.

Lord, we know the most empathetic Person ever to walk the planet was Your Son, Jesus Christ. Help us to see as He sees, listen as He listens, and care as He cares. Help us to show empathy by caring about each other's concerns and feeling what each other feels. Help us enter their world so we can rejoice when they rejoice and mourn when they mourn.

DAY 58

Trustworthy

All you need to say is simply "Yes" or "No"; anything beyond this comes from the evil one.

Matthew 5:37

I learned early on in my marriage not to make many promises to my wife. This may sound odd—if there's any person on the planet you should make promises to, it should be your spouse, right? But one day early on in our marriage, I told her, "Kristen, I promise I will be home by 6:00 p.m." I got busy at work, talked to a coworker about a relationship issue, and then started walking to my car at 6:15. I got home around 6:45, forty-five minutes after I promised Kristen I'd get home.

Kristen is not a strict rulekeeper, but she rightly expressed her frustration that I didn't keep my promise. Even though I wasn't engaging in some gross sin, I didn't keep my word to her. I wasn't precise in my communication and commitments, and in the process, I hurt my wife. I learned early on only to make promises to Kristen if I knew I was willing and able to keep them. It has helped me choose my words more carefully, and it's increased trust in our marriage.

In the most famous sermon Jesus ever preached, the Sermon on the Mount (Matt. 5–7), He taught on major topics such as marriage, divorce, praying, anger, and much more. In Matthew 5:37, He said, "All you need to say is simply 'Yes' or 'No'; anything beyond this comes from the evil one." In other words, keep your promises—be trustworthy. It's easy to make an oath or a promise; it's a lot harder to keep it. For this reason, I encourage you not to make empty promises so that you can be a trustworthy spouse.

I do want to give you one big caveat. In your marriage vows, you are going to make some big promises. Keep those promises! For example, I promised to Kristen that I would not divorce her. I also promised to be faithful to her. I will actively fight to keep her as my standard of beauty for the rest of my life.[1] God keeps His promises. You and I should do the same.

> *God, thank You that You always do everything You say You're going to do. You're worthy of our trust. You are who You say You are, and You do everything You say You're going to do. Help us to be the same way in marriage. We pray that we would be a man and woman who do and say trustworthy things. Help us to be quick to confess when we fall short, and help us to keep our promises.*

DAY 59

Caring

Instead, we were like young children among you. Just as a nursing mother cares for her children, so we cared for you. Because we loved you so much, we were delighted to share with you not only the gospel of God but our lives as well.

1 Thessalonians 2:7–8

In 1 Thessalonians, the apostle Paul challenged the Thessalonian believers to hold firm to their faith in the midst of persecution. He exhorted them to move forward in their faith and encouraged them to remain steadfast. In 1 Thessalonians 2:7, he compared the way he cared for them to a mother's care for her children. Paul's tone was tender toward these believers as he said he was delighted to share with them not just the gospel of

Jesus Christ but also his life. His love and care for them seemed genuine and sacrificial.

When we care for someone, we look after their needs to make sure they're protected from harm. We seek to make sure they make wise decisions and have what they need to survive and thrive. Many people in our world care only for themselves. I admit I often find myself thinking of my own cares and needs before anyone else's. It's selfish, and our world is marked much more by uncaring and selfish people than caring and selfless people.

In marriage, you get the amazing privilege of caring for your spouse. This starts right now in your relationship, before you even say "I do." You can help bear your future spouse's burdens or navigate challenging relationships with parents or in-laws. You can help them make decisions as you plan your wedding. And you can pray for their needs, worries, and concerns.

This privilege carries forward into marriage as you start your lives together as newlyweds and make a million big and small decisions about your home, jobs, and cars. If you raise children, you get to care for them by selflessly serving them when you're exhausted and when the diapers stink and you can both fall asleep standing up!

Lord willing, the occasions to care for your spouse will continue to old age as you help each other stand up and walk when you're weak in physical strength. You'll be able to make sure your spouse takes their medications, and you'll serve one another when the kids are gone and the grandkids come to visit.

Marriage will provide you with more opportunities to care for another human being than any other relationship on this planet. What a joy to get to stand out from the rest of our self-ish, uncaring world.

> *Lord, we have a simple prayer request today: please help us to care for each other. Will You please show us one way today that we can better care for each other? And please give us the courage to do whatever You show us. Thank You!*

DAY 60

Vulnerable

Therefore confess your sins to each other and pray for each other so that you may be healed. The prayer of a righteous person is powerful and effective.

James 5:16

One of the scariest and most vulnerable moments in life is when we confess our sins to the Lord and to other people. When we confess, we plead guilty to sin. We admit and agree with the Lord that we've fallen short of His glory and perfection. But when we confess, we open the door for others to pray for us.

It takes courage to admit our sins and struggles to others. When we're authentic, we show a congruence between what we say about ourselves and what we do and who we are. We're consistent in every part of our lives. But when we're vulnerable, we take it to the next level, because we risk getting hurt or rejected. When we admit our weaknesses, we don't know how others will respond. They could mock us, reject us, or choose to gossip about us.

The marriage relationship is the place where you should be freer than any other relationship. When you're naked without shame with your spouse (Gen. 2:25), you ought to be able to be completely honest and open about yourself. God has created marriage so that we can be known without fear of rejection. But it takes courage and vulnerability to open ourselves up to others.

Here are a few ways you can choose to be vulnerable with your signficiant other, both before and after you say "I do."

- *Share your hopes and dreams.* Don't be afraid to share your hopes and dreams with each other. Marriage ought to provide a safe space for you to put your gifts to work!
- *Confess your fears and insecurities.* If you're anxious about a work conversation, worried about becoming a parent, or embarrassed about something you said or did, share with your spouse.
- *Ask for prayer.* Our prayers give us great insight into where we need the Lord. Pray with your spouse, and ask them to pray for you.

Lord, we pray we would be completely honest and transparent with each other. Help us create the kind of marriage in which we're not afraid to admit and confess when we fall short. Help us not to fear rejection when we're vulnerable. And most of all, thank You that You don't reject us. Rather, we're fully known and fully loved by You. Help us to do the same with each other.

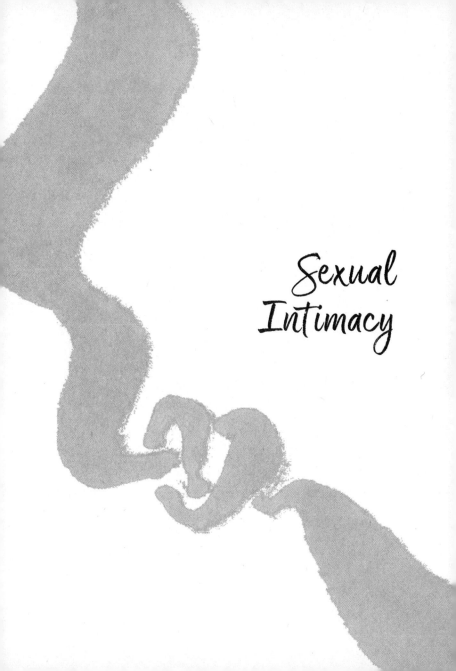

Sexual
Intimacy

DAY 61

Pure

Flee from sexual immorality. All other sins a person commits are outside the body, but whoever sins sexually, sins against their own body.

1 Corinthians 6:18

Sometimes people think purity exists only for teenagers who are trying not to cross physical boundaries with a boyfriend or girlfriend. Other times people talk about purity as something to keep singles from looking at pornography. It's as if purity is only for people who aren't married.

But this couldn't be further from the truth. All followers of Christ are called to live lives marked by purity. Paul wrote in 1 Corinthians 6:18 that we are to "flee from sexual immorality."

While all sin separates us from God, sexual sin typically carries with it more significant consequences in this life. This is why Paul went on to say that all other sins a person commits are outside the body, but sexual sin is against one's own body. Sexual misconduct tends to have significant consequences, and for this reason Paul encouraged all Christians to flee from sexual immorality. He clearly wanted all believers to be spared the devastating consequences of a lack of purity.

The good news for you as you get ready to be married is that marriage will allow you to enjoy the gift of sexual intimacy with your spouse. You'll get to experience the joy and pleasure God intends for a husband and wife. But even after you say "I do," you're still called to live a life marked by purity. God longs for you to be self-controlled and to stay pure in your thoughts and actions. This means you and your significant other shouldn't look at others with lustful intent (Job 31:1; Matt. 5:27–28). Pornography is out of bounds, and any sexual activity in any way, shape, or form with someone other than your spouse is immoral and impure.

I love my wife and want to honor her and honor the Lord in every way. But purity has always been a challenge for me in marriage. While I haven't acted inappropriately with any other woman, I still struggle at times with lustful thoughts. Through movies, TV, or in real life with women I see, my purity is challenged by temptations. I work very hard to protect my eyes and thoughts, and it's a daily battle to fight for purity.[1] Most men and many women struggle in similar ways. Fight for purity and pursue it in your marriage and in your relationship with Christ. It's worth it.

> *God, we pray You will help us in this battle. The world does us no favors, and we're surrounded by temptations everywhere we look. We need You to help us win in this area of our lives and marriage. Please help us to be pure in our thoughts and actions, knowing it's worth it to fight hard for Your glory and our good.*

DAY 62

Free

It is for freedom that Christ has set us free. Stand firm, then, and do not let yourselves be burdened again by a yoke of slavery.

Galatians 5:1

What if I asked you, right now, to give your phone to your significant other, along with the passwords for all of your accounts? Would you be willing to let your future spouse look through your personal emails and text messages? Could they look at your search history? Your direct messages on Instagram? Is there anything on your phone you wouldn't want them to see?

Some of you read the questions above and are terrified. You don't want your significant other to see what you've said, texted, or seen. You're petrified of what they'll find. You'd rather throw your phone in the closest lake. You're trapped in a prison of fear right now.

Others of you are willing to give your significant other your phones right now, along with your passwords, search history, and access to your messages. You're willing to do the same thing with your laptop and your tablet or e-reader too. You have nothing to fear. You are free, and it's the best feeling in the world.

I so badly want you and your significant other to be free. When we hide, we live in fear of getting caught. We lie to hide lies to hide more lies. It's a miserable existence. I know because I've lived there. I've experienced seasons of freedom and then found myself "burdened again by a yoke of slavery," as Paul described in Galatians 5:1. Paul was right. It's a burden to be enslaved to sin, and hiding struggles is flat-out exhausting.

Instead, I pray you would be free. I pray you and your significant other would have nothing to hide, and you'd be quick to confess when you fall short. None of us is perfect—there's only One who is perfect, and His name is Jesus. You will sin, over and over and over. So choose to be someone who quickly confesses to your spouse and others so that you don't become locked in a proverbial prison of guilt and shame.

> *God, give us the courage to be open and honest with each other when we fall short. Help us to confess our sins to You and to each other. And help us each show grace to the other when they fall short. Thank You that, because of the sacrifice of Your Son, Jesus, we can find freedom in our relationship with You. Thank You for freedom in Christ and for Your promise that "there is now no condemnation for those who are in Christ Jesus" (Rom. 8:1).*

DAY 63

Innovative

To the weak I became weak, to win the weak. I have become all
things to all people so that by all possible means I might save some.

1 Corinthians 9:22

I want you to protect your mind from wandering to inappropri-
ate thoughts before you get married, but today we're going to
think through what it looks like to be innovative, both inside
and outside the bedroom. Married couples can get stuck in ruts,
so it's important that you consider and pray about how to be
more innovative as a couple.

In 1 Corinthians 9:22, Paul said he was willing to become all
things to all people so that some may be saved. He was willing to
be weak, he was open to new experiences, and he would probably even have cheered for a team he didn't like to help build a

relationship with a nonbeliever. So what can we learn from Paul about marriage, romance, and sexual intimacy?

Just as Paul was willing to innovate to reach some, we should be willing to be innovative in marriage to protect us from boredom. When couples are bored, they often look outside of marriage for fun with someone of the opposite sex who's not their spouse. This is often how affairs begin. It's never an excuse and never makes it right, but it's far too often a reality. Instead, look for ways to build creativity and innovation in your marriage.

The bedroom should never involve others outside your spouse (Matt. 5:27–28). This means no pornography or other people. You should never hurt someone against their will or desire (Phil. 2:3–4). Rather, put their needs before your own needs. And you should never do anything with your spouse that violates either of your consciences (Rom. 14). Outside of that, there's all kinds of freedom to innovate and have fun in marriage, in and out of the bedroom. Be willing to try new things. Keep things fresh and fun. Within the bounds of your future marriage, you can enjoy the gift of sex "for the glory of God" (1 Cor. 10:31).

> *God, help us to be innovative in our future marriage. You love fun and innovation—You created the world and created us, and we're evidence of it. Help us to enjoy the gifts You've given in marriage, including sexual intimacy. We pray we'd always give You the glory for this amazing gift. Please help us to steward it well and to enjoy the gift of marriage. And before we say "I do," will You please protect us from crossing boundaries physically? We need Your help, so we humbly ask You for it.*

DAY 64

Self-Controlled

For the Spirit God gave us does not make us timid, but gives us power, love and self-discipline.

2 Timothy 1:7

God's Word has a lot to say about self-control. Proverbs 25:28 says a person without self-control is "like a city whose walls are broken through." Paul listed "self-control" as a fruit of the Spirit in Galatians 5:22–23. In 1 Timothy 3:2 and Titus 1:8, Paul said church elders are to be "self-controlled." And in 2 Timothy 1:7, Paul said the Spirit God gave to followers of Jesus Christ "does not make us timid, but gives us power, love and self-discipline."

God gives us the power to be self-controlled. It's not something we try to muster up on our own. Self-control is not white-knuckling it when faced with temptations. We don't have to live in constant fear that we're going to fail in our attempts to be self-controlled. Yes, there's a part we must play—we must be the ones who say no to temptations—but God gives us the power through His Spirit to be self-controlled.

You and your future spouse will face many challenges when it comes to self-control. You may be tempted to get drunk, binge on food, or watch countless hours of Netflix. You will need to help each other with your temptations. One of the most beautiful parts of marriage is that in addition to His Spirit, God gives us a companion who can help us when we're most tempted.

I want to focus on one specific area of self-control: lust and pornography. We're all bombarded with sexual images on Instagram, online, and wherever we go in life. It's a battle many people face to differing degrees. It's been a struggle for me since I was eleven years old. I understand the battle, and thankfully, since God's Spirit gives me self-control, it's been an area of victory in my life.

But I've watched this struggle destroy hundreds of marriages. I've seen pornography creep into a husband's or wife's life and consume them. I've seen it lead them to be dissatisfied sexually with their spouse. And I've seen it lead men and women to passivity as they no longer pursue their spouse romantically or sexually.

The temptation is not the problem; it's what you do with the temptation. Have you and your significant other discussed any struggles you may have with lust and pornography? Before you say "I do," this is a conversation you must have. It's something you should pray about constantly, because the battle is real, and we need all the help and self-control we can get.

Lord, we absolutely need You in every way, and specifically we need You to help us be self-controlled in every part of our lives. Help us to depend on Your Spirit to lead and guide us and to help us be self-controlled in the face of temptation. Thank You that when we are tempted, You "provide a way out," as Paul said in 1 Corinthians 10:13, and You give us Your Spirit to help us.

DAY 65

Resilient

> But if you do marry, you have not sinned; and if a virgin marries, she has not sinned. But those who marry will face many troubles in this life, and I want to spare you this.
>
> 1 Corinthians 7:28

The only promise about marriage in the entire Bible is found in 1 Corinthians 7:28, where Paul said if you marry, you "will face many troubles in this life." He didn't promise you an easy marriage, amazing sex, great kids, and happily ever after. Paul even tried to warn us by saying he wanted to spare us the troubles that come our way when we marry.

Sometimes you'll be the one who brings the trouble. Your own sin struggles (such as people-pleasing, selfishness, and lust) will challenge your marriage. Other times your spouse's struggles will lead to trouble. Sometimes the troubles you face will come from outside your marriage (such as in-laws or job issues), and other times it's no one's fault (such as infertility). Regardless, you will face challenges.

How will you and your future spouse handle the adversity you are promised to face in marriage? How will you walk together through the trials, struggles, and challenges of life?

The resilient marriage learns from Jesus's half brother James. In James 1:2–4, he wrote, "Consider it pure joy, my brothers and sisters, whenever you face trials of many kinds, because you know that the testing of your faith produces perseverance. Let perseverance finish its work so that you may be mature and complete, not lacking anything."

Specifically, I've seen many couples face trials in the bedroom. This particular struggle often comes as a surprise to couples, and it requires resilience to work through these challenges. Most couples are embarrassed to admit or discuss problems with sexual intimacy, so it requires even more resilience to seek help from your community, a pastor, or a biblical counselor.

If you're not resilient in your marriage, you'll want to quit whenever you face adversity. You may hang in there a few times, but when the challenges keep coming, you or your spouse will look for a way out. Something resilient bounces back into its original form when it faces stress or tension. The resilient couple perseveres and "bounces back" through trials and challenges. They're guaranteed to come your way, so stay strong and be resilient when you face trouble.

> *Lord, we truly need You. Help us to stay strong when we face trials in our marriage. Help us to stand strong when trouble comes. Help us to be gracious and patient with each other and endure difficulties as Your Son, Jesus, endured. We know trials are coming our way, so we pray we wouldn't be surprised and would bounce back even stronger after enduring trials together.*

DAY 66

Loving

We love because he first loved us.

1 John 4:19

The word *love* is overused in our culture—"I love coffee," "I love college football," "I love jelly beans"—but often underpracticed in marriage. We enter marriage with loving feelings but often forget or choose not to live out loving actions after we say "I do." The word *love* is easy to say but difficult to apply.

But you can be a loving spouse from day one of marriage. The Bible says, "We love because he first loved us" (1 John 4:19). As we follow in Christ's footsteps, we are to love others in the same way He loved us. While we don't die on a cross for the sins of others, we do follow His example of how to love. Jesus should be our model of what it looks like to love others.

If you've been to a wedding, you've no doubt heard 1 Corinthians 13:4–7. In this well-known passage, Paul wrote, "Love is patient, love is kind. It does not envy, it does not boast, it is not proud. It does not dishonor others, it is not self-seeking, it is not easily angered, it keeps no record of wrongs. Love does not delight in evil but rejoices with the truth. It always protects, always trusts, always hopes, always perseveres."

I love (pun intended) the following exercise: reread 1 Corinthians 13:4–7, and anytime you see the word *love* or a reference to love, plug in your own name. For example, "Scott is patient, Scott is kind. Scott does not envy," and so forth. Do you embody these aspects of love? Are you patient and kind? Do you envy? Are you self-seeking? Do you keep a record of wrongs or a list of rights? Do you protect, trust, hope, and persevere? Ask your significant other if you live out these aspects of love, and take a moment to encourage your spouse-to-be for the ways they love you well. For example, in verse 5, Paul said that love is not self-seeking. I recently shared with my wife how selfless she is with her time. I'm consistently encouraged by the list of errands she runs every day for the benefit of others.[1]

When we do these things from 1 Corinthians 13, we love our spouse well. And we do this because Christ first loved us.

God, we pray You'd help us always to love each other. Help us not to cheapen love to the pattern of the world but rather love as You love. We pray we'd love because You first loved us and that our love for others would come from Your love for us. Help us to live out 1 Corinthians 13:4–7 in the way we love each other as husband and wife.

DAY 67

Glad

Shout for joy to the LORD, all the earth. Worship the LORD with gladness; come before him with joyful songs.

Psalm 100:1–2

We have a gladness problem in marriages today. Between high divorce rates in and out of the church and couples who are still married but miserable, marriage does not look appealing to a watching world. A single friend of mine recently said he knew of very few compelling reasons to get married—why should he want to do it? My heart sank a little when he shared that all he typically heard from married people was how hard marriage was, and he heard very little about the greatness of marriage. Christian married couples often lack joy.

The psalms are filled with reminders and encouragement to sing for joy and to be glad. In Psalm 100:2, the psalmist said, "Worship the LORD with gladness." Psalm 90:14 shares a similar sentiment: "Satisfy us in the morning with your unfailing love, that we may sing for joy and be glad all our days." Yet too many Christians today walk around filled with gloom and doom instead of joy and gladness. It's especially true of many Christian marriages. It's no wonder young adults aren't drawn to marriage!

This is a good time for you to evaluate how glad you and your significant other are in your relationship. It doesn't mean you're argument-free. It doesn't mean you don't struggle from time to time. Rather, are you glad to see each other? Do you miss each other when you're not together? As you think about the future, do you get excited about spending the next fifty years together? Do you anticipate excitement and gladness when you think about being intimate with each other?

One of the areas of marriage where we can rejoice and be glad is in the bedroom. Sex is a great gift from a God who loves us. He made sex pleasurable and fun. He gives us a lot of freedom to enjoy each other and explore each other's bodies. There are times when sex can make you laugh hysterically together—we can enjoy sex "for the glory of God" (1 Cor. 10:31). When you serve each other and enjoy the gift of physical intimacy, it ought to make you glad for the gift of marriage.

God, please help us to look different from the many couples around us who seem miserable together. Help us to be filled with gladness so our lives would be a testimony to Your great love for us. You give us everything we need in life, including the beautiful gifts of marriage and sexual intimacy. May we always reflect Your joy and be glad as we worship You.

DAY 68

Initiating

But God demonstrates his own love for us in this: While we were
still sinners, Christ died for us.

Romans 5:8

A godly spouse isn't afraid to initiate. So often the easier thing
to do is to sit back and wait. But a spouse who initiates goes
first and does whatever needs to be done for the benefit of the
relationship. Here are a few examples of what initiating looks
like in a marriage:

- *Confess first to God and then to your spouse.* Godly
  spouses know the truth of Proverbs 28:13: "Whoever
  conceals their sins does not prosper, but the one who
  confesses and renounces them finds mercy." They don't
  wait until they get caught but rather initiate by confessing

first and then renouncing their sins by changing their habits and patterns.

- *When you see a problem, fix it.* For example, don't haggle over whether it's their dirty plate or your dirty plate, just wash it.
- *Initiate romance and sex with your spouse.* Take the initiative to love and serve your spouse in physical intimacy.

My wife does this better than any other human being I know. She serves without ceasing and initiates romantically, spiritually, relationally, and so much more. A spouse who initiates brings their spouse joy.

As we initiate love with our spouse, we follow in the footsteps of Jesus, who initiated on our behalf. In Romans 5:8, Paul said that for followers of Christ, His example is everything we need to see. Jesus didn't wait until we were good or clean enough. Rather, He demonstrated His own love by dying for us. Fully aware of our past, present, and future sins, Jesus still chose to initiate love on our behalf. May we initiate for our future spouse's benefit in the same way.

God, please help us serve our partner well. Help us each to put the needs of the other first and to see things from their perspective. Help us to initiate for each other's benefit and to the glory of God. Please allow us to not keep track of rights and wrongs but rather to initiate selflessly. Thank You that You didn't wait for us to clean up our act but rather chose to initiate love by dying for us when we didn't deserve it.

Parents
and In-Laws

DAY 69

Secure in Identity

For we are God's handiwork, created in Christ Jesus to do good works, which God prepared in advance for us to do.

Ephesians 2:10

Anytime we meet someone new, we typically ask that person a few questions:

- What's your name?
- Where are you from, and where did you grow up?
- What do you do for work?
- What do you like to do with your free time?

For example, "My name is Scott. I live in Waco, Texas, and I was born in Hackensack, New Jersey. I am a marriage pastor.

In my free time I like to hang out with my family, and I like to write." We take all these responses and many more and make them part of our identity. *I am a runner. I am a college football fan. I am a singer.* And so on.

Our family of origin shapes much of our identity. The things our parents said to us and about us help define how we view ourselves. For example, if your dad told you how much he loved you and how much more the Lord loves you, then you might have a secure identity. On the other hand, if your dad told you that you were worthless, lazy, annoying, and stupid, then you might struggle with how you view yourself and how you think God sees you.

As followers of Christ, we have a much more important legacy. We are children of the King, redeemed and saved. God chose us before the beginning of time to be His followers (Eph. 1:4). Paul even says we are "God's handiwork, created in Christ Jesus to do good works" (2:10). Our most important identity is that we are God's beloved children and we are His handiwork.

This is a paradigm shift for many of us, since we tend to place our identity in so many external factors, such as our family of origin. We have last names to help identify our family. Many of these ways we identify ourselves are important, but they're not ultimate.

The attribute of identity plays an important role in marriage because you and your future spouse constantly need to remember where your identity lies. You will face temptations to think lowly of yourself in marriage when you mess up. Your spouse may belittle you with their words. You may find yourself in a codependent relationship with your spouse. And while your marriage is the most important human relationship on earth, it will never be your most important relationship. For this reason, your identity needs to be securely tied to the Lord and not to anything or anyone else.

> *God, it's easy to place our identity in stuff, titles, marital status, job, family of origin, and so much more. We know the world places a high premium on status and titles. Help us to find our greatest identity in being Your workmanship and being a son and daughter of the King. Help us consistently to remind each other what's right and true about our identities.*

DAY 70

Curious

After three days they found him in the temple courts, sitting among the teachers, listening to them and asking them questions.

Luke 2:46

My friends Nate and Jackie[1] stick out when it comes to conversations. Both are experts at asking great questions. While most of us like to talk about ourselves, these two friends of mine do the best job at listening to others by asking insightful, thoughtful questions. They're curious to learn more, and in the process they put the other person before themselves. This kind of listening requires a maturity most people don't have, and I always walk away from conversations with either of them encouraged.

Jesus, even though He was omniscient, showed this same kind of curiosity as a young boy when He asked questions of those older than He was. As always, Jesus modeled the type of life we want to follow. And as a reminder, the purpose of this book is not only to teach you great ways to grow your marriage but also to encourage you to become more like Jesus. One specific way to become more like Jesus is to ask questions and live a life filled with curiosity.

This trait will also pay big dividends in your future marriage, since curious people take the initiative to learn more about their spouse. I recommend this practice with your family and in-laws as well. Early on in our marriage, I remember asking my father-in-law questions about his US Navy experience and flying background. He's wired very differently than I am, so asking questions helped me better understand his story and strengthened our relationship.

Furthermore, asking questions and being curious will be a tremendous benefit if you have kids someday. You'll find that if you have multiple children, each one will be unique. Ask questions to better understand your children. Be a learner. If you or your future spouse are bringing children into your marriage from a prior relationship, asking questions will also help you build relationships with stepchildren.

Most of us spend too much time thinking about ourselves. Seek to learn more about others by being curious and asking great questions.

Lord, help us to be learners about each other. Help us to do the same with others—friends, parents, in-laws, and our (future) children. We pray we'd be students of each other by asking good questions and seeking to understand how You made each of us with unique personalities and strengths. Thank You that You know us perfectly and completely, and we pray that through curious hearts we'd come to better know each other.

DAY 71

Courteous

Remind them to be submissive to rulers and authorities, to be obedient, to be ready for every good work, to speak evil of no one, to avoid quarreling, to be gentle, and to show perfect courtesy toward all people.

Titus 3:1–2 ESV

Over the years I've learned to be observant of how couples treat each other in public. I've watched husbands and wives pay more attention to their phones than to their spouse on date nights. I've seen men open car doors for their kids but not their wife. I've noticed one spouse using an umbrella and not offering cover for their spouse when they're walking in the rain. And I've noticed several nonverbal ways couples communicate with each other. (It's usually not very pretty.)

As a whole, human beings have lost the art of courtesy in relationships. When we're courteous, we show respect to others. We're polite, kind, friendly, and considerate. We consider others more important than ourselves, and we're well-mannered toward others. In Titus 3:1–2, the apostle Paul challenged his readers to be peaceable, considerate, and gentle toward others. The English Standard Version says we are to "show perfect courtesy toward all people."

Imagine what your relationship would be like if you were always courteous to your significant other. I believe a marriage marked by courtesy stands out—it pops. Instead of being marked by selfishness, what if your marriage was characterized by thoughtfulness and consideration of your spouse?

Here are a few ways you and your significant other can show courtesy to each other:

- When you get up to get a drink, ask your significant other if they'd like something.
- When they get home with groceries, help bring the bags inside.
- When they talk to you, put down your phone and look them in the eyes.
- Ask them how you can specifically pray for them.
- Wash their dishes for them.

None of these suggestions ought to be earth-shattering or groundbreaking. Rather, they're all small ways to show courtesy to one another.

Lord, courtesy seems like a forgotten art in relationships. Help us in marriage to consider first the needs and desires of our spouse. Help us to be courteous of the other's needs and desires instead of focusing on what we want. We pray our courteous marriage would be marked by thoughtful consideration of each other.

DAY 72

Peaceable

If it is possible, as far as it depends on you, live at peace with everyone.

Romans 12:18

When you dreamed of what your future spouse would be like, *peaceable* probably didn't make your list. Humble? Yes. Attractive? Yes. Fun? Yes. But peaceable? More than likely it wasn't an attribute that came to mind. Yet I promise you that you will long for a spouse who does whatever they can to pursue peace in your home, family, and marriage.

The world is marked by strife. Financial issues, disease, politics, war, and much more divide our world. And even inside the home, many families are marked by yelling, arguments, sibling rivalry, and more. Relationships marked by peace are an answer to prayer. Do you have a friend who tends to bring calm into the chaos? I have several friends who, when the world seems to spiral out of control, bring a sense of calm and peace to the room.

Some dear friends of mine became pregnant in 2021 with their third child. As you can imagine, they were thrilled! A few months into the pregnancy, they found out their baby girl would not live long outside the womb. They grieved as any couple would, but they also fought for unity in their marriage and in their love for the Lord. I was amazed at the way they walked through this crisis with "the peace of God, which transcends all understanding" (Phil. 4:7).

A peaceable spouse will do everything they can to fight for peace—"as far as it depends on you," said Paul (Rom. 12:18). A couple of chapters later, in Romans 14:19, he said, "Let us therefore make every effort to do what leads to peace and to mutual edification."

Today, pray that your life, your spouse, and your marriage will be marked by the type of peace that

- initiates when there's unresolved conflict, disregarding who is at fault (Rom. 5:8).
- surpasses all understanding and will guard your heart and mind in Christ Jesus (Phil. 4:6–7).
- brings order instead of chaos and disorder (1 Cor. 14:33).
- is gentle and calm amid a chaotic and divisive world (John 16:33).

God, thank You for giving us the perfect picture of peace in Your Son, Jesus Christ. Thank You that while the world around Him was marked by sin, chaos, and division, He did everything He could to model peace. Help us to be peaceful spouses who do everything we can to bring peace to our home. We pray that a sense of peace would pervade our relationship and our family. Thank You for being our Good Shepherd who brings peace even in the darkest valleys (Ps. 23:4).

DAY 73

Cooperative

How good and pleasant it is when God's people live together in unity!

Psalm 133:1

I made a promise to myself that I would always strive to be honest in my writing. This means at times I have to share the not-so-great moments of marriage. This very day I had one of those moments. Tomorrow morning, we're throwing a graduation/eighteenth-birthday party for our twin sons. It's going to be a great celebration, and friends and family are gathering to celebrate our boys.

But during our preparations for the party, I have not been a great husband. I've felt sorry for myself for having to run errands, clean the house, and order food for the party. I'm tired and emotional about the party, since I know we only have a few more weeks with our twins before they leave to work at camp. Kristen is even more tired and probably more emotional about our twins leaving.

Today, instead of working as a team, Kristen and I argued. We each had our own opinion about what should be done and how to do it. Instead of discussing things calmly, we argued and snapped. Finally, I just left the house and told her I didn't want to be home. Not my finest hour, and I'm not proud of my actions and words. At that moment, we weren't being united as a husband and wife working together but rather were two selfish people arguing for their own way (especially me). We were not living together in unity!

The couple who cooperates well will lean into and seek to engage in conflict management and resolution. They'll work together on chores and yield to the other's needs and preferences. They'll take on hard projects together and help each other become more like Jesus Christ. They'll be united when working through challenges with their family of origin and in-laws.

This idea of cooperation reminds me of teamwork in sports. As I am writing this, the NBA playoffs are in progress. I'm not much of an NBA fan, but I do love watching how a great team works together. The best teams realize the importance of each position and the necessity of teamwork. The best team members cooperate with each other. It's the same in marriage. You and your significant other should become a championship team who cooperates with each other.

> *Lord, we want to be a team who works well together. Help us not to compete but rather cooperate with each other as husband and wife. Help us to live out our one-flesh relationship that You have designed. When we fall short, help us own it quickly and be examples of how a husband and wife are to cooperate in marriage.*

DAY 74

Kind

Therefore, as God's chosen people, holy and dearly loved, clothe yourselves with compassion, kindness, humility, gentleness and patience.

Colossians 3:12

In Colossians 3:12–17, Paul described the spiritual clothing followers of Christ should put on. In the beginning of the chapter, he described the actions and attitude believers are to take off, but starting in verse 12, he told us what "clothes" every Christian should wear. This new outfit, when worn by a husband or wife, will help your marriage more than you realize. One of the most important pieces of this new outfit is kindness.

We often hear the word *kindness*, but do we know what it really means? When someone is kind, it means they are friendly and considerate to others. A kind person is sympathetic, honest, listens well, and is eager to help. Paul said, "Love is kind" (1 Cor. 13:4), and "kindness" is listed among the fruit of the Spirit in Galatians 5:22–23. Paul also said it's the kindness of the Lord that leads us to repentance (Rom. 2:4). God's Word is filled with verses highlighting the importance of kindness.

Since kindness is important to all relationships, think of how very important it must be in marriage. In a tough world that tends to reward cutthroat ambition, we should remember all the more just how necessary kindness is between a husband and wife.

What does kindness look like in marriage?

- It could be as simple as treating your spouse as you want to be treated. Put their needs before your own and encourage them every day.

- Kindness doesn't just involve words but should extend into actions. For example, in Acts 28, the people of Malta showed hospitality and kindness when they greeted Paul and the others who were shipwrecked by being welcoming and starting a fire.

- Encourage each other with kind words that are "sweet to the soul and healing to the bones" (Prov. 16:24). Be generous with words of affirmation toward your spouse. We need all the encouragement we can get (Heb. 3:13).

- You can show kindness to your spouse through thoughtful, creative gifts. You know your significant other better than anyone else—what gift would be a kind encouragement to them?

As you get dressed tomorrow morning, make sure you put on kindness, and find a specific way to be kind to your significant other.

Lord, thank You for the kindness You show us. It's Your kindness that has led us to turn away from our sins and toward You. Help us to be kind to others, especially each other. We pray we'd put on compassion, humility, and kindness every day of our lives. Since we are among God's chosen people, help us joyfully put on kindness toward each other.

DAY 75

Hopeful

May the God of hope fill you with all joy and peace as you trust in him, so that you may overflow with hope by the power of the Holy Spirit.

Romans 15:13

You and your future spouse will hope for many things in marriage. You may hope for a thriving marriage, kids who love Jesus, a nice home, and great friends. You will have many dreams and desires for your life together as husband and wife. Some dreams will be stated and shared, while others will be hopes you didn't even know you had.

Not all your hopes will come to pass. If the Lord gives you kids, they won't always love you or love Jesus. Your job, friends, and car will all let you down. You'll find cracks in the wall from a shifting foundation, your air conditioner unit will go out in the middle of the summer, and you won't be able to keep up with all the weeds in your yard.

More importantly, your spouse is likely going to disappoint you at times. They may not keep all their promises, and they probably won't do everything the way you'd do it. Your future in-laws, as much as you love them, may frustrate you at holidays and family get-togethers. At times you might even wonder if you made the right decision to get married. And guess what? Your spouse will feel the same. You'll likely let down your spouse, and your spouse will probably wonder the same thing. We cannot place our hopes in each other.

If you put your hope in anyone or anything other than Jesus, you will experience hurt and disappointment.

For this reason, it's crucial to put your hope, not in your spouse, money, or kids, but in the Lord. Your only true hope in this life is in Jesus Christ. He will never let you down, and He will never disappoint you. He's "the same yesterday and today and forever" (Heb. 13:8). He's your "living hope" (1 Pet. 1:3)—all day, every day.

> Lord, help us to place our hope in You and You alone. It's so easy to hope in the things of this world or in people, specifically each other. We know we're going to disappoint each other, so help us place our hope in You. Thank You that You give us reason to hope and that You never let us down. You are our living hope. Help us to remember that every moment of every day.

DAY 76

Servant-Minded

For even the Son of Man did not come to be served, but to serve,
and to give his life as a ransom for many.

Mark 10:45

Few things will serve your marriage more than being servant-minded. Our fleshly natures and the world around us do all they can to help us worship the kingdom of self. Statements like "Have it your way" and "You deserve it!" will echo in your earbuds and over the radio. However, Christian marriage calls us to serve our spouse.

When you are married, you will have countless opportunities to serve your spouse every day, from the moment you wake up until the minute you fall asleep. You will get the privilege of serving your spouse in the kitchen and in the bedroom. No other human relationship gives us more opportunities to serve another person over decades of life than marriage.

The challenge you'll face is that you'll often want your spouse to put your needs before their own. You'll get home from work and think your spouse ought to think about your day and your needs. And they'll do the same, which creates a problem since you both think the other should serve you.

Your family of origin plays a huge role in helping shape your expectations of service in marriage. If you watched your mom and dad do this well, then you will more than likely be servant-minded in marriage. If, on the other hand, your parents did not model serving each other well, then serving your spouse will seem like a foreign concept.

On an average day in married life, you'll get to help around the house by doing laundry, shopping for groceries, cooking dinner, cleaning the bathroom, and so much more. You will dislike some tasks, and your spouse will as well. But the godly, servant-minded spouse will joyfully serve their spouse and do whatever needs to be done around the home. Often you will serve and never be noticed. But when you serve your spouse, you become more like Jesus Christ.

In Mark 10:45, Jesus said that He "did not come to be served, but to serve." Isn't that incredible? No other human ever deserved to be served more than Jesus, the Son of God. But He laid down His rights and demonstrated how to serve others.

How can you follow in Jesus's footsteps and serve your significant other, both today and after you get married?

Heavenly Father, please help us to be servant-minded toward each other. Please help us to joyfully put the needs of each other first and to give with no expectation of return. Help us do the things our spouse doesn't like to do and serve with a selfless, sacrificial attitude. Thank You for the example of Your Son, Jesus, who served us by giving His life for us. Help us to serve others, first and foremost our spouse.

Friendship and
Romance

DAY 77

Devoted

Do not merely listen to the word, and so deceive yourselves.
Do what it says.

James 1:22

Spend a few minutes with someone, and you can probably tell
what or who they're devoted to. Take a look at their calendar,
credit card statement, or search history, and you know what or
who is most important in their life. For example, if you spent
any time with me, you'd know I care a lot about books, college
sports, and food. I probably care a little too much about *The
Office*, coffee, and listening to podcasts.

At the same time, I hope you could tell I love Jesus because I
read my Bible, pray, and serve His church and His people with
the gifts God has entrusted to me. I also hope you'd be able to

tell I am fully devoted to my wife and our marriage because of how much time we spend together, how we serve on mission as a couple, and how much fun we have as a couple and a family.

To be devoted to someone is to be loving and loyal to that person. It's giving a large part of your time and resources to that individual. If your marriage is important to you, then you will be fully devoted to your spouse. You'll do whatever you need to do to make your marriage the most important relationship you have outside your relationship with Jesus. You don't just know about marriage; you do what God's Word says and fight for full devotion.

Too many couples settle for a "good enough" marriage. They compare their marriage to their parents', friends', or what they see on TV and think they're doing fine—and that's good enough. I don't want you to settle in marriage. I want you to be fully devoted to your spouse.

Do you want your marriage to be strong and healthy? Then choose not to settle and simply be good enough. I believe you want a great marriage. So fight for it and be devoted to Jesus and devoted to your future spouse.

> God, we see the marriages of the world, and we don't want to be like most couples around us. Help our marriage to be a right reflection of Your devotion to us and of Your design and intention for marriage. Help us to know what Your Word says, and help us not to deceive ourselves but rather to do everything Your Word says. We need You to help us be fully devoted to You first and then to each other.

DAY 78

Playful

There is a time for everything . . . a time to weep and a time to laugh, a time to mourn and a time to dance.

Ecclesiastes 3:1, 4

Before a couple says "I do," they typically have all kinds of fun. They pursue each other creatively and are adventurous and fun. Hormones like dopamine and norepinephrine course through your bodies when attraction kicks in and you both like each other. I remember the giddiness I felt in the beginning of my relationship with Kristen. We enjoyed running together, trying new restaurants, and exploring all over Atlanta. We were so playful. We laughed a lot—the kind of playful laughter where you laugh until you cry.

But when you get married, things start to change. You start paying bills, organizing your stuff, and mowing the lawn. Your life begins to fill up with nonstop trips to the grocery and home improvement stores. With no malicious intent whatsoever, many couples eventually stop having fun together. It becomes even more challenging when kids are added to the mix. Children easily become the center of your lives, and you have a lot less time to be playful in marriage.[1]

Laughter and play are so important in marriage. We need to look for ways to keep the spark alive and keep those hormones running through our bodies. As life becomes more complicated and busy with chores, bills, jobs, and kids, we will need to prioritize fun in marriage.[2]

Just because you'll soon be a married adult doesn't mean you still can't play and have fun together. Play will change as your life changes, so be intentional to figure out what's fun for you as a couple. Seek to serve your spouse by doing things they enjoy. How do you like to play, and what makes you laugh? Take a moment to discuss fun as a couple and commit to doing something playful together this week.

> *Lord, we pray we'd always steal each other's hearts in marriage. We pray we'd have fun, laugh until we cry, and make memories together. Help us never to get too old to have fun together. We pray we will serve each other well and be intentional to seek what our spouse enjoys. Through the fun we have together, we pray others would want to know more about who You are.*

DAY 79

Supportive

Therefore encourage one another and build each other up, just as in fact you are doing.

1 Thessalonians 5:11

Every one of us needs help in unique and different ways. Some of us need emotional help. Others of us need an attaboy or an attagirl. Some of us need tough love, and others just need a listening ear. We all need support and help, and that looks different for every one of us.

We see early in the Bible that "it is not good for the man to be alone" (Gen. 2:18). He needed some help and support, so God made for the man a suitable helper. This is, of course, a two-way street in that women also need help, so the man also helps the woman. The husband and wife get the privilege of supporting each other in countless ways.

In my marriage, I'm the more emotional spouse, and I'm much more dramatic too. Kristen is much steadier emotionally than I am, and I'm the one who cries. As I'm writing this, our twin sons are about to graduate from high school, and I'm all kinds of emotional. Kristen supports me by comforting me when I want to cry. Kristen is also much more serious than I am. I support her by bringing laughter to the home and by reminding her to relax at times. We make each other better as we support each other.

What are some other ways you can support your significant other?

- *You pray for them.* You know where they need help, so you intentionally pray for God to comfort and help them.
- *You create space for them.* You want them to succeed in life, so you create space and margin for them to do well in their job or whatever role God gives them.
- *You serve them.* You should know your spouse better than any other person on the planet, so you can serve them in specific ways because you know exactly what they need.
- *You listen to them.* You take time to ask good questions, and you listen to their responses to those questions.

In Matthew 22:39, Jesus said the second greatest commandment is to "love your neighbor as yourself." You have no closer neighbor than your spouse. When you know and love your significant other both now and in your future marriage, you are supporting them in their unique needs.

> *Lord, we confess we're so often focused on our needs and desires that we miss out on serving those around us. Specifically, we know we can miss out on the needs of our future spouse. Help us to encourage and build each other up, and may we be supportive of each other in all that we say and do as husband and wife.*

DAY 80

Healthy

Do you not know that your bodies are temples of the Holy Spirit, who is in you, whom you have received from God? You are not your own; you were bought at a price. Therefore honor God with your bodies.

1 Corinthians 6:19–20

When Kristen and I started dating, we helped each other stay healthy. We ran together almost every day after work, and we'd eat healthy meals when we tried new restaurants. I worked hard to impress Kristen—it was fun spending time with her, and, to be honest, I wanted to look good so she'd like me. We made a great team, and I knew we'd be willing and able to help each other honor God with our bodies.

In 1 Corinthians 6:12–20, Paul addressed the church in Corinth about their sexual sin. He ended the chapter by reminding the Corinthians their bodies had been bought at an extremely high price. What was the cost? The death of God's one and only Son, Jesus. In exchange for this infinitely high price, God challenges us to honor Him with our bodies (v. 20).

This challenge to honor God with our bodies is related not just to sexual sin but to everything connected to the body. This means it matters how we eat, sleep, and exercise. It means we shouldn't intentionally harm ourselves, and we need to be cautious of any addictive substance because of what it can do to our bodies.

As you prepare for engagement or marriage, pay attention to how well (or not well) you're choosing to honor God with your body. Do the same with your future spouse. Do you have similar views on sleeping, eating, and exercising? Have you discussed your views on drugs and alcohol? You might just assume you're aligned with each other, but it would be wise for you to discuss this so that you're not surprised after you get married.

To be transparent with you, staying healthy has been my biggest struggle in life. I love unhealthy foods, and I've been overweight most of my life.[1] I like to exercise, but I only exercise so that I can eat more. I tend to work too much, so I compromise on how much sleep I get every night. Fortunately, this is something Kristen helps me with, and we work on it together. When you get married, you'll be one flesh with each other (Gen. 2:24). Help your spouse honor God with their body as you seek to honor Him with your own.

> *God, we want to honor You with our bodies. We know You bought us at the highest possible price—the life, death, and resurrection of Your Son, Jesus. Help us to make wise and healthy decisions about how we eat, sleep, and exercise. We pray we'd partner with each other well so that we would honor You with our bodies and our lives.*

DAY 81

Cherishing

You have stolen my heart, my sister, my bride; you have stolen my heart with one glance of your eyes, with one jewel of your necklace.

Song of Songs 4:9

I love the language in the book of the Bible called the Song of Songs. The way the man and woman in this book speak to and about each other challenges me to up my communication game in my marriage. Their poetic language captures the love story between a man and a woman in such a way that you want to be in love like this couple. Some of it may not sound so flattering to our modern ears, but when you understand the original language, it becomes quite endearing. For example, husbands, I would not suggest that you tell your future wife, "Your hair is like a flock of goats descending from the hills of Gilead" (Song 4:1). But in the original Hebrew language, this was a beautiful praise. (For you, just tell her that her hair looks and smells nice!)

Throughout the Song of Songs, we see the man and woman cherish each other with their words. Many couples use the word *cherish* in their marriage vows, but they may not take the time to understand what it really means. In his book *Cherish: The One Word That Changes Everything for Your Marriage*, Gary Thomas said, "A cherishing attitude will enrich, deepen, and spiritually strengthen your marriage."[1] *Cherish* is one of my favorite marriage books because of how well the author encourages the reader to cherish their spouse. When we cherish our spouse well, we turn marriage from an obligation to a delight.

Thomas went on to say, "To cherish something is to *hold it dear*. That means you think about it, and when you do, you feel great pleasure. You have great affection for it."[2] A Christian marriage ought to be marked by this kind of affection, where your spouse won't need to question where your affection and attention lie. When you and your future spouse cherish each other, you won't have to worry about your spouse falling in love with someone else, and you can rest with security and confidence in your love for each other.

When you cherish your significant other, you take an interest in what interests them. You take notice of the things that impact them in positive and negative ways. You see them, and they feel known and valued. Too many marriages lack the trait of cherishing, and when they do, the marriage falls apart or slowly fades to misery. When we cherish our spouse well, they know they're the only one for us.

God, help us to hold each other dear, to take notice of what the other values, and to help them flourish and grow in their relationship with You. Help us joyfully embrace the gift of marriage and the spouse You've given us. As we often hear in wedding vows, may we love and cherish each other "till death do us part."

DAY 82

Adoring

My beloved is mine and I am his; he browses among the lilies.

Song of Songs 2:16

The next time you go out for dinner, look around at the married couples in the restaurant. I'll bet they look at their phones more than at each other. During the week, they probably communicate with each other primarily via texts and DMs. They got married because they adored each other. But a few years into marriage, they've gone from adored to bored. How did they get there?

In chapter 2 of the Song of Songs, the love between the man and woman grew and intensified. They praised each other's character and appearance, and they expressed deep admiration and longing for each other. They were eager to see each other and desired to become one flesh in marriage.

In verse 16, the woman said, "My beloved is mine and I am his." They belonged to each other. They completely adored each other. It's the kind of adoration that when seen in others kind of sickens us—it seems so cute and adorable but unattainable. Deep down, we long to adore our spouse and to have them adore us. We want our spouse to plan romantic dates. We want to talk and laugh until we cry. We want to know we're valued, longed for, and desired. And in Song of Songs, we see a beautiful picture of this longing played out in real life.

The challenges of marriage and the tough nature of life will wear any of us down. Your spouse can do something no other human being can do—they're able to cut through the challenges and discouragement and speak life and acceptance into you. When we adore our spouse, we lovingly admire them and are unconditionally devoted to them. This adoration provides a level of security and peace we all need. We don't fear our spouse leaving or harming us when we adore each other in this way.

A former boss of mine and his wife do a lot of marriage teaching together. They have a great marriage, so they lead with integrity. They've got a lot of experience teaching, so they teach with gravitas. They're funny and have great stories, so they keep the audience engaged. But one of the things that sticks out about them is the way the wife looks at her husband during their teaching. You can tell my friends adore each other. You can't watch them teach and not notice their mutual adoration. I pray the same can be said of you and your future spouse!

God, we know You adore us. The only reason You would send Your Son is out of Your selfless love and adoration for us. We pray this very same posture would dominate our relationship. We pray that we would adore each other and that our love would be secure, since we know it's founded in Your love for us.

DAY 83

Intentional

Be very careful, then, how you live—not as unwise but as wise,
making the most of every opportunity, because the days are evil.

Ephesians 5:15–16

There never seems to be enough time in the day. Between responsibilities at work, at home, and in the key relationships in our lives, we always seem to run out of time. We forget to do errands or lack sufficient hours in the day and intentionally choose not to get everything done. We desire to spend more time in our most important relationships, but time escapes us.

If you neglect your marital relationship, you'll have a bigger problem on your hands than if you skip some errands. We need to be intentional about what we say yes and no to, and we need to be careful how we live. We want to live "not as unwise but as wise" (Eph. 5:15). In your marriage, you will not naturally move toward a healthier, stronger relationship with your spouse. Without intentional effort, you will not grow in emotional, relational, spiritual, or physical intimacy with your spouse. And the enemy would love nothing more than to see you drift apart in your marriage.

When you and your spouse are intentional in marriage, you make decisions with intent, meaning you choose wisely and carefully how to spend your time, money, energy, and resources.

Here are some ways you and your future spouse can be intentional in your relationship, even before marriage:

- *You discuss how to prioritize your relationship.* You know time is limited and options for spending it are infinite, so you make the marriage relationship your most important one (outside of your personal relationship with the Lord).
- *You make the time to communicate and manage conflict.* Challenges are inevitable, but intentional spouses make it a priority to communicate and handle conflict well.
- *You take time to pray together (much like you're doing in this book).* You know you need help from the Lord to face the challenges you'll encounter on a daily basis. Consistently ask God to help you and seek to grow your relationship with the Lord.

There are countless ways to be intentional in your marriage. You and your significant other can decide today to intentionally pursue each other and pursue the Lord together.

God, our time is limited, and we want to make the most of the time we have together. Help us to be intentional in our marriage—to grow our friendship and to grow in intimacy. Help us to discern what to say yes and no to. We know that without intentional effort, we won't move toward You or toward each other, so we humbly ask You to help us intentionally pursue You and each other.

DAY 84

Fun

Enjoy life with your wife, whom you love.

Ecclesiastes 9:9

I've worked in full-time marriage ministry for more than seventeen years and have ministered alongside hundreds of couples who have mentored and cared for thousands of premarried couples. A few years ago, I asked four hundred of these leaders, "What's your favorite part of marriage?" The number one answer, by a landslide, was companionship. Leaders responded with words like *companionship*, *teammates*, *friendship*, *fun*, *playmate*, and others.

When you look at married couples, it may not always look like they enjoy being married to each other. Many couples appear to merely tolerate each other. So how is it possible that so many couples said companionship, friendship, and fun are their favorite aspects of marriage, while so many married couples around us seem miserable and stuck? The difference is that the leaders I asked were healthy and thriving couples who were mentoring other couples. Most married people you see probably aren't serving other couples. Could it be that the biggest difference between healthy couples and bored couples is that the healthy ones know how to enjoy each other in marriage?

As a couple who is preparing for marriage, you may find it hard to believe you would ever feel stuck or bored with each other. But I've seen it play out so many times: couples who were fun before marriage get stuck in a rut after marriage. This certainly happened with Kristen and me in different seasons of life, such as when we had four kids under the age of five and when we were financially strapped.

I hope that you and your significant other will always pursue fun and friendship in marriage. Here are a few ways you can do this well, both before and after you say "I do."

- Choose to pursue hobbies together.
- Continue to go on dates with each other.
- Put your phones down and communicate with each other.
- Ask each other questions and never cease being a student of your spouse.
- Hang out with other fun couples who will help you grow your marriage.

What sounds fun to you? Your definition of *fun* might be completely different from your significant other's, but look for ways to enjoy each other today.

God, we pray we'd have fun together as a couple. Help us be best friends with each other, laugh until we cry, and creatively pursue each other all the days of our lives. Show us how to enjoy life together and to bring You glory through our fun and friendship. Help us to make friends who will help us have fun. You are the author of fun, and we're grateful that we're made in Your image and likeness.

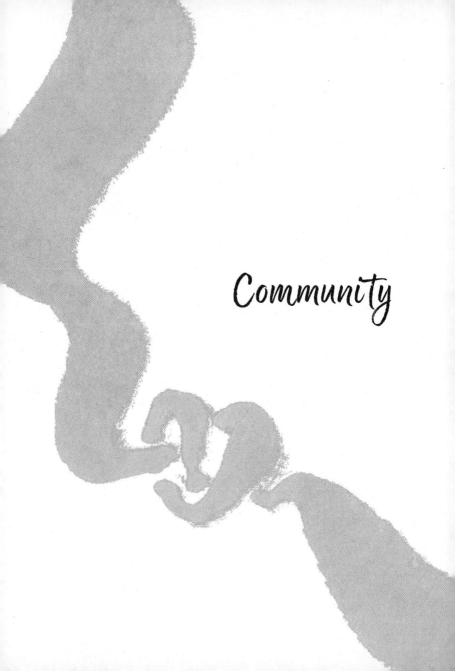

Community

DAY 85

Community-Centered

Walk with the wise and become wise, for a companion of fools suffers harm.

Proverbs 13:20

Sometimes marriage feels like one decision after another:

- "What should we have for dinner?"
- "Should we buy this TV or that vacuum cleaner?"
- "How should we discipline our child?"

At times, it's just exhausting! Decision after decision after decision.

Chances are that you and your spouse-to-be have different perspectives on many questions you're trying to answer. And while you may discuss your decisions with each other, there will be many occasions when you need to widen the circle and include others. A community-centered marriage includes others in the celebrations and challenges of life. For this reason, it's crucial to walk through life with wise friends.

Proverbs 13:20 is both a promise and a warning: If you walk with the wise, you will grow wise. But if you hang out with fools, you're going to suffer harm. As a married couple, you will want to choose your community carefully, since your friends will often be on the front lines of decisions you make and arguments you enter together.

What do I mean by *community*? Almost every church has a form of community—Sunday school, small groups, and many other names and styles. Your community is a group of like-minded followers of Christ with whom you have a mutually beneficial relationship, helping one another become more like Jesus Christ. A healthy community is authentic, biblical, and committed to one another's growth.

As mentioned above, a community-centered marriage can help you make wise decisions. Ideally, your community will include single friends, newlyweds, and mentor couples who are further down the road of life. This community of fellow believers can help carry your burdens, celebrate the wins of life, and manage conflict when you both think you're right. They can challenge you to grow spiritually and hold you accountable when you want to grow in specific areas.

Kristen and I decided when we got married never to live life apart from a community of fellow believers. Our single friends helped us grow when we were single, and we committed to live married life with other married couples. "Bad company corrupts good character" (1 Cor. 15:33), so make sure you walk through life with others who will help you grow Christlike character.

> *God, we pray we'll have a community-centered marriage. Help us to make great friends who love Jesus and love others. Please help us to avoid isolation in every season of our marriage. We know it's not good for us to be alone—we acknowledge our desperate need for You and for others. We pray now for the fellow believers You'll bring into our lives. Help us to be great friends to them and vice versa.*

DAY 86

Patient

Whoever is patient has great understanding, but one who is quick-tempered displays folly.

Proverbs 14:29

Kristen and I have been a part of a church-based community group with other married couples for all the years of our marriage. We were in a group with newlyweds when we were newlyweds. After that we joined a group with couples married a similar number of years and with kids around the same ages. All told, we've been a part of four different groups and have led a handful of groups with young couples. One consistent factor among all our groups is that it requires patience to be in community with others.

People can be challenging and difficult. I'm challenging and difficult. You and your significant other are challenging and difficult at times. It's one thing we all hold in common. Therefore, we need to learn how to be patient with each other. We'll cheer for different teams, have different Enneagram numbers, vote for candidates in different parties, and have different sin struggles. We need to learn how to be patient with others.

In 1 Corinthians 13:4, the apostle Paul said, "Love is patient." Patience is a part of the fruit of the Spirit for followers of Christ (Gal. 5:22–23). We are to clothe ourselves with patience—it ought to be part of our daily spiritual wardrobe (Col. 3:12–13).

Your marriage will require you to be patient with each other and patient with your community of friends. There will be times when you and your future spouse will not agree with each other, and you'll need to bring others in to help you make a decision. When you do this, it will go much better for you if you're patient and display great understanding rather than being quick-tempered.

When Kristen and I lived in Dallas, we were in a community group in our church with four other married couples. We met every other week with this same group of couples for more than thirteen years. We laughed a lot, we processed many decisions together, and we even worked through disagreements from time to time. I'm thankful for the patience and understanding these four couples showed Kristen and me, and hopefully we did the same for them.

Patience and understanding will serve you well in your relationship with friends and in your marriage. We need all the patience and understanding we can get, so ask the Lord to help you and your significant other be marked by patience.

> *God, on our own we tend to be selfish and impatient. We want what we want when we want it, and we don't want to wait. God, help us to be patient in our marriage. Help us to resist being quick-tempered and instead be marked by patience and great understanding.*

DAY 87

Persevering

Let us run with perseverance the race marked out for us, fixing our eyes on Jesus, the pioneer and perfecter of faith. For the joy set before him he endured the cross, scorning its shame, and sat down at the right hand of the throne of God.

Hebrews 12:1–2

One of the biggest concerns I have when looking at younger generations is that when the going gets tough, young people often quit. Yes, my generation has the same challenge, but the tendency to quit seems to be increasing in younger generations. Many people have lost the willingness to persevere when things get tough.

The Bible often describes the benefits of persevering through challenges. When something is repeated several times in different books of the Bible, I especially want to pay close attention. James 1:2–4 says when we face trials, we are to persevere through them so that we can grow in character. In Romans 5:3–4, Paul said suffering leads to perseverance, which leads us to grow in character and hope.

In Hebrews 12:2, we are commanded to fix our eyes upon Jesus. He endured the cross and persevered through the biggest injustice in the history of the world. Remember, the goal of this book is not just to grow your marriage; it's to help you become more like Jesus Christ. So keep your eyes fixed on Him and take note of everything He does.

In her book *Grit: The Power of Passion and Perseverance*, Angela Duckworth talked about this characteristic. People who possess grit are determined, tenacious, and persevere in life. She said that those who possess grit succeed in life.[1] My friends at Pine Cove Camps defined *grit* as "doing what is hard to do, to be who you want to be."[2]

I've seen the same thing hold true in marriage. Couples who are determined, work hard, don't give up when trials come, and persevere in the ups and downs of life tend to thrive in their marriage. You will face trials in marriage—it's guaranteed. Paul said, "Those who marry will face many troubles in this life" (1 Cor. 7:28). Agree right now, even before saying "I do," that the two of you will persevere in the trials of life.

> *God, we know we're going to face trials and challenges in life. We pray You'd help us to persevere in them. Help us never to quit and always to fight for our marriage. We pray we'd follow the perfect example of Jesus, who endured the cross and persevered until the very end. We pray we will do the same in our marriage.*

DAY 88

Marked by Integrity

Now this is our boast: Our conscience testifies that we have
conducted ourselves in the world, and especially in our relations
with you, with integrity and godly sincerity. We have done so,
relying not on worldly wisdom but on God's grace.

2 Corinthians 1:12

My family and I live in Waco, Texas, home of the Baylor University Bears. In Waco, most people cheer for the Bears. But because Waco is only ninety minutes from Austin and ninety minutes from College Station, it's not uncommon to see University of Texas Longhorns and Texas A&M Aggies fans too. You might also see fans of Texas Tech Red Raiders and SMU Mustangs. What you will not see, however, is someone who's a die-hard Baylor fan also cheering wholeheartedly for the Longhorns or Aggies. It would be confusing to see someone root for both teams.[1]

When we're divided in our affections, it's as if we have divided hearts. Instead of giving someone our full devotion, our affections are split. When we do this, we lack integrity and are not whole. Merriam-Webster defines *integrity* as "the quality or state of being complete or undivided."[2] When our actions don't align with our words, we're divided and lack integrity.

You may make a promise to your future spouse or one of your close friends, but when you fail to keep that promise, you lack integrity. If you're a leader in the workplace, but you're passive when you come home to your family, you lack integrity. If you don't cuss in front of your kids, but you cuss like a sailor in front of your spouse, you lack integrity.[3]

Can you see why integrity is so important in marriage? When you make your marriage vows, you're making giant promises to your significant other. I've benefited from like-minded followers of Christ helping me grow in integrity. They've helped me keep my promises to my wife and kids and held me accountable to having hard conversations with coworkers.

You want to have the integrity to follow through on what you promise with your family, in your neighborhood, and in your job. To do this will require God's grace, as Paul shared in 2 Corinthians 1:12: "We have conducted ourselves in the world, and especially in our relations with you, with integrity and godly sincerity. We have done so, relying not on worldly wisdom but on God's grace."

If you want a marriage characterized by integrity, ask God to help you, because we all tend to lack integrity by being inconsistent in different roles in our lives.

God, we pray You'd help us to be filled with integrity in marriage. Help us to keep our promises and to do what we say we're going to do. If we struggle with integrity, help us to be quick to confess to our spouse and to others. We know it's confusing to a watching world when a Christian marriage looks just like a worldly marriage, so would You please help us to be complete and whole in You? Please help us when we're tempted to do something different from what we said we're going to do.

DAY 89

Wise

If any of you lacks wisdom, you should ask God, who gives generously to all without finding fault, and it will be given to you.

James 1:5

Life is filled with decisions. *What school should I go to? What job should I take? Should I rent or buy?* Not to mention all the relationship decisions you need to make. You've made many decisions to get to where you are today, but the choices will never end. Planning a wedding is filled with them, and life as a married couple will provide endless opportunities to make decisions.

I consider myself to be a simple guy. Even though I have two master's degrees, at the end of the day I naturally gravitate toward simplicity. For this reason, I ask God for wisdom multiple times every day. I love James's challenge to his readers in James 1:5. He said that when we lack wisdom, we should turn to the Lord. As followers of Jesus, we know He gives generously—He desires to give us wisdom even more than we desire His wisdom.

God finds no fault in us when we ask Him for wisdom, and He generously provides it to His children. But we must *ask* Him for that wisdom. I encourage you, starting today, to be a couple who leans not on their own knowledge and wisdom but rather leans on the Lord.

- When you need wisdom in working through communication and conflict challenges, ask God for wisdom.
- When you're deciding whether or not to start trying to grow your family, ask God for wisdom.
- When you're choosing between visiting his family or hers for Christmas and Thanksgiving, ask God for wisdom.
- When you're choosing where you will go to church, how you'll serve the body of Christ, and how much and where to give financially, ask God for wisdom.
- When you're choosing which couples you will spend time with as you build community with other newlyweds, ask God for wisdom.

God is infinitely wise, and He longs to help you grow by providing wisdom from above. Be humble and ask Him for it.

God, You promise to provide wisdom to us generously and without finding fault. We pray that in our marriage we would consistently turn to You—that we would be dependent upon You for wisdom, and that we wouldn't lean on our own understanding (Prov. 3:5). We can't trust ourselves at times. We need You, so when we need to make decisions, help us to be a couple who comes to You as the source of all wisdom. Thank You for generously providing it.

DAY 90

Confessing

Whoever conceals their sins does not prosper, but the one who confesses and renounces them finds mercy.

Proverbs 28:13

Our natural tendency is to hide the things about ourselves we're not proud of. We don't want others to know about our shopping or browsing habits or secret addictions. For years, I hid a struggle with pornography from everyone. My pornography addiction embarrassed me, and I didn't want anyone to know about it. I lived in fear of others finding out, and I consequently struggled in every facet of my life.

A few years after trusting in Christ as my Savior, I finally confessed my porn struggle to a small group of other Christian men. Hiding my sin wore me out, and I had to let others in so I could start to find some victory and healing. My group encouraged me for sharing, and they offered to help me in this battle. When I finally confessed and renounced my sin, I found mercy.

In marriage, you'll have opportunities just about every day to confess your sins and struggles to your spouse. Healthy married couples regularly and consistently take time to confess to each other. The problem comes when individuals act as if they have nothing to admit to each other. We know we "all have sinned and fall short of the glory of God" (Rom. 3:23), so why would we ever pretend to be without sin?

I encourage you and your spouse-to-be to make confession to each other a regular habit in marriage. Confession requires humility, since you must be willing to admit you fall short. Show forgiveness to each other as you hear confession and agree to attack your struggles together. Maintaining a regular habit of confession in your marriage will allow you to live with each other and be naked without shame (Gen. 2:25).

Admitting your sins to someone else is hard work. It's often embarrassing and shameful to admit when you've fallen short. And as hard as it is to confess, it's often even harder to hear a confession from your spouse. But it's much better to confess and work through the challenges than to hide your sin or get caught.

I was recently reminded of God's grace through confession in the lives of two friends. The wife had an affair years ago but was convicted of her sin. She confessed to her husband, and the two worked through the challenges with the help of their church, close friends, and a biblical counselor. Today, their marriage is better than ever, the wife works in full-time ministry, and they serve together in their church's marriage ministry. Spouses who confess and renounce their sins find mercy (Prov. 28:13).

> *Lord, thank You that You show us mercy when we confess and renounce our sin to You. We pray we'd do the same for each other in marriage. Help us humbly to admit when we fall short and to cultivate the type of marriage where we can safely confess sin to each other. May Your grace toward us in our confession never cease to amaze us, and may we show mercy toward each other in confession.*

DAY 91

Discerning

And this is my prayer: that your love may abound more and more in knowledge and depth of insight, so that you may be able to discern what is best and may be pure and blameless for the day of Christ.

Philippians 1:9–10

Life is filled with decisions. Just think about all the decisions you've made in your relationship so far:

- Should I ask them out?
- Should I say yes?
- How do I know if they're the one?
- How do I act when I meet their parents for the first time?

- Should we serve dinner at our wedding? Alcohol? Who do we invite? Where is our honeymoon going to be?

The list goes on and on.

Every married couple will tell you that you're just getting started on making decisions. For this reason, you and your significant other need to be discerning. The newlywed years can be filled with more big financial decisions than any other season of life. You'll make choices about cars, jobs, homes, kids, jobs again, church, investments, and so much more. Your decisions no longer affect only yourself. Every decision you make affects your future spouse too, compounding the need for wisdom and discernment.

In Philippians 1:9–10, Paul told us we must be able to discern what's best to demonstrate our love for the Lord and to help us become most like Jesus Christ. As you and your future spouse spend your lives together, you'll need to learn how to choose what's best from many good options. Most decisions you'll make will not be black-and-white but filled with many shades of gray, making the need for discernment even greater. And when you make tough decisions, you open the door for potential conflict between you and your spouse.

You've already made many big choices in your relationship. Learn to depend more and more on God's Word, His Spirit who leads you and guides you, and the people He's surrounded you with. You have all you need to make good decisions, especially as you ask the Lord to help you become increasingly more discerning (2 Pet. 1:3).

God, we need You every minute, every hour, and in every decision. Help us to become more discerning as individuals and as a couple so that we can choose what's best. Please help us to make good choices when we're stuck between two good options. Help us to trust You as You help us to become discerning like Your Son, Jesus.

DAY 92

Truth Telling

Then you will know the truth, and the truth will set you free.

John 8:32

Some good friends recently walked a hard road in their marriage. The husband was in graduate school, and he started to struggle in his classes. Without telling his wife or any of their friends, he dropped out of school for the semester. The same thing happened the semester after that. He hid the truth from everyone as he pretended to be a full-time grad student. When his wife found out he was hiding the truth, she was completely and understandably devastated.

In John 8:32, Jesus said when you know the truth, the truth will set you free. On the other hand, for the enemies of the Lord, whose father is the devil, there is no truth (v. 44). When we hide the truth from others, including our spouse, we lack freedom and act like an enemy of the Lord. Jesus desires for us to live in freedom with our spouse and with others.

One of my biggest challenges in interacting with others is that I sometimes dance around the truth. Since I struggle with being a people-pleaser, I often share things with others in a way that makes me look better. I avoid speaking directly about issues because I care too much about what people think. In the process, I avoid speaking the truth.

But as followers of Christ, there's no room for avoiding the truth. This especially holds true in marriage. God has created the one-flesh marriage relationship to be a safe place for sharing the truth and for being honest with each other. Even when it's hard to say, we owe it to each other to be truthful and honest. God gives us a spouse in part to help sharpen us so that we can become more like Jesus Christ. When we avoid speaking or listening to truth, we're impairing our ability to become more like Christ.

By God's grace, the couple I referenced above is doing well in their marriage. After the husband's lies came out, he started down the path of restoring their marriage. He opened himself up for others to ask hard questions, he apologized to and asked for forgiveness of everyone he wronged, and he resumed working on his master's degree. His wife and friends recently celebrated his graduation. Even more important, he's experiencing freedom now, because truth sets us free!

One of the greatest gifts in marriage is being able to be fully honest, transparent, and truthful with one another. Are there any areas of your relationship in which you have not been truthful with your significant other? If so, confess and start living a truthful life today.

> *God, everywhere we look we see a lack of honesty and integrity. Help us to be truth tellers in our marriage. Help us to avoid telling lies. Instead, we pray our lives and our marriage will be filled with truth. Thank You that the truth sets us free.*

Parenting
and Kids

DAY 93

Sees Children as a Blessing

Children are a heritage from the LORD, offspring a reward from him. Like arrows in the hands of a warrior are children born in one's youth. Blessed is the man whose quiver is full of them.

Psalm 127:3–5

Before we had kids, I really wanted to be a dad. Kristen and I talked at length before marriage about our desires to be parents one day. I cried tears of joy when I found out we were having twins! But I have a confession to make: I did not like being a dad the first five years of my kids' lives.

I know you're not supposed to say stuff like that, but when our sons were babies and toddlers, they were anything but a blessing to me. They didn't cooperate with what I wanted them to do. They cried, pooped, cried, screamed, cried, whined, and cried all the time. Did I mention they cried all the time? They cost me money, time, and sleep. Instead of seeing them as a gift or blessing, I saw them as a burden.

I have another confession: I was wrong in my view of children! My biggest problem was not my children but rather how much they revealed sin and selfishness in my heart.

Thankfully, now I believe our four sons are among the greatest blessings in my life. But during those early years, my selfishness prevented me from being a joyful, content parent. I missed out on the blessing of being a dad because I was blinded by my sin. As my kids grew up, I started to love being a dad. They brought me joy. I loved cheering them on in soccer games and laughing until I cried when we had tickle fights. I'm watching them grow into young men who love Jesus and love others. They became a blessing to me. I wish I hadn't resented those early years.

Some of you are bringing kids into your marriage from prior relationships. Some of you are terrified of having kids. Some of you want to get pregnant on your honeymoon, and others want to wait years until you welcome kids into the world. Some of you will foster or adopt children. And some of you will have deep sadness because you're not able to conceive. Regardless of where you fall in these situations, you'll want to make sure you and your future spouse have the same view about kids. Pray and discuss when you want to start trying, how many kids you want to have, and what you'll do if you're unable to conceive. And if you have kids from a previous relationship, talk through the dynamics of your blended family.

As you pray about growing your family, seek wisdom from the Lord. Ask Him to help you be unified as a couple about children. They truly are a blessing and gift from the Lord.

Lord, if You choose to bless us with children, we pray we would be great parents and would love the children You entrust to us. If You choose not to give us children, help us be content and serve You faithfully. May we be unified in our view of children, that we would see them as a blessing from You. If we add children to our family, may we cherish the gift of being parents and enjoy every minute we get in raising children. Help us to love them as You love us.

DAY 94

Missional

For the Son of Man came to seek and to save the lost.

Luke 19:10

What does it mean to live a life that is missional? For the follower of Jesus Christ, it means that you are all about God's mission; you undertake an important task He has assigned to you as His follower.

We need to be all about God's mission while we're on earth. God has given every believer at least three assignments: the Great Commission—to go and make disciples (Matt. 28:19–20), the Great Commandment—to love God and love others (22:37–40), and the challenge to seek and save the lost (Luke 19:10). If this is God's mission for each believer on earth as an individual, then it only makes sense that this also would be His mission for you as a couple. The missional marriage is in sync with God's mission for us as individuals.

If you want to live on mission as a couple, you need to know God's mission for your life and live it out together as husband and wife. In so many ways, God can multiply your efforts as a husband and wife and as parents. He can use you in greater ways as a family to serve others and share your faith. You can complement each other in your gifts as you seek to be on mission in marriage and as a family.

Kristen and I love getting to serve together, and we strive to use our gifts to serve others well. We live on mission in our family by opening up our home to friends and neighbors, by discipling newlyweds, and by giving financially to our church and other Christian ministries. Our kids are involved in everything we do while we serve on mission together.

A great conversation to have before you get married is about how you'll view your family. You'll either spend all your time inwardly focused, or you'll see yourselves as a family who lives on mission. God wants to use your marriage and your kids for His glory and for the good of others. A family that is strong and honors Him will communicate to the world about the goodness of God. A Christian couple whose family isn't worth emulating becomes a stumbling block to a watching world.

God, we pray our marriage and family will point others toward You. We pray that our marriage will be worth emulating and that You'll help us to be on mission for You together. We know that it's easy to gravitate toward bigger homes and nicer stuff. Help us not to make such things our goal but instead to establish that our goal and hope in marriage will be centered around You and Your mission for our lives.

DAY 95

Selfless

What causes fights and quarrels among you? Don't they come
from your desires that battle within you?

James 4:1

No one ever had to teach me how to be selfish, and no one ever
had to teach me how to argue over what most benefits me. My
wife and I never had to teach our sons how to fight over LEGOs.
And I never had a class that told me to take the larger half of
a cookie when I split it with someone else. We see something
we want and go after it. In the process, our selfish desires reign
supreme.

In 2004, I loudly declared to Kristen that I thought my life
was effectively over because my baby twin sons wouldn't cooperate with my desires. I needed to get some work done, and their

constant crying was driving me crazy.[1] In that moment I had no concern for my children or for my wife. All of life had become about *my* desires, wants, and needs. (We're all selfish enough as it is, but it becomes amplified when we add kids to the mix.)

Selfishness will destroy a marriage. When we get married, we become one flesh with our spouse (Gen. 2:24), so what happens to one person directly impacts the other, in both the good and the bad. It directly impacts your children as well. When a husband and wife struggle, often the people most affected are their children.

Selfishness is the opposite of what God desires in a Christian marriage. A God-honoring, selfless marriage calls you to give, serve, and put the needs of your spouse before your own. Selfishness, on the other hand, puts your needs first, second, and third, and doesn't pay attention to or care about your spouse or your kids.

James 4:1 says, "What causes fights and quarrels among you? Don't they come from your desires that battle within you?" In this passage, James tells us we fight because we are selfish. At its root, we don't argue because of money, schedules, kids, sex, or anything else. Those might appear to be the drivers of the issue, but the real causes of our disagreements are the selfish desires that war within us. When we don't get what we want, we argue with each other.

A few years ago, I journaled every day for six months a brief paragraph of how my selfishness was affecting my life and marriage. I didn't realize just how significantly it was impacting my relationships with others, including my spouse and kids. I'm not suggesting you have to journal every day about your selfishness, but I suggest paying attention to how selfish desires lead you to argue with your future spouse. Selfish desires also affect the way you parent. Your children become an inconvenience rather than a blessing (see day 93). Instead, choose to be selfless in your relationship—and someday also in your marriage.

> *God, please help us see where we're selfish. We pray that our relationship wouldn't be marked by selfishness but rather by selflessness. Help us to see where selfish desires lead to problems in our relationship. Please help us see areas where we could be more selfless in the ways we serve each other. Help us have "the mind of Christ" (1 Cor. 2:16), who selflessly gave His life so that we could live. May He always be our example and goal.*

DAY 96

Creative

> So God created mankind in his own image, in the image of God
> he created them; male and female he created them.
>
> Genesis 1:27

In the creation account recorded in Genesis 1 and 2, God created
man and woman in His image and likeness. Both you and your
significant other were created in the image of God! The kids
some of you are bringing into marriage and the kids you may
have in the future are also created in the image of God. The very
God who created colors, mountains, beaches, and everything
beautiful on our planet created us. The Lord formed the man
from the dust of the earth (2:7) and created the woman from a
rib He pulled from the man (v. 22).

Sometimes we break up the world into people who are creative and everyone else. We think musicians, artists, painters, and writers are creative types, and everyone else on the planet lacks creativity. That's just not true. If the creative God of the universe made each of us in His image and likeness, then by definition we're all creative. This means you are creative, and you're marrying someone who is also creative.

But when you look around, you'll see marriages that appear boring. Husbands and wives seem like they'd rather watch TV together than do something adventurous. They don't go on date nights or do anything fun with each other—all they do is talk about kids, work, and bills. But it doesn't have to be this way. As people created in the image and likeness of God, you are filled with creativity. And while you do need to work, raise kids, and pay bills, your marriage should be marked by a whole lot more.

What if you parented in creative ways? Some of you have kids now, and many of you want kids in the future. Is it your hope and desire to be creative and intentional in the ways you make memories and lead your kids? Do you both want to be creative in conversations around the dinner table and adventures you take as a family?

We've loved celebrating the creativity in each of our four sons, and it looks different in each of them. One son is creative in his fun-loving personality, one is creative in his songwriting and guitar playing, one is creative in the way he trains to be a better athlete, and one is creative in the ways he entertains our family with voices and imitations. We love seeing how God has creatively formed each of our sons.

Take a moment to think about how that affects your relationship. What if you celebrated the unique aspects of your future spouse and your present or future children? Because both you and your significant other are creative, your relationship and family could and should be creative as well. This will look different for every couple, so I can't prescribe what it must look like in your marriage. But don't get stuck in the rut, thinking you're not creative. Don't forget: God crafted you in His image and likeness, so live your marriage and family in light of His creative nature.

Lord, thank You for creating us in Your image and likeness! You are creative, and You create beautiful things— You make everything beautiful in Your time (Eccl. 3:11). We pray that our marriage and family would be marked by creativity, that we wouldn't be boring, and that every day would be an adventure as we creatively pursue You, each other, and our (future) kids.

DAY 97

Flexible

When they came to the border of Mysia, they tried to enter
Bithynia, but the Spirit of Jesus would not allow them to.

Acts 16:7

In Acts 16, Paul and his companions wanted to go one way,
but the Lord led them a different direction. They may have had
friends expecting them, venues lined up for speaking engage-
ments, and dinner reservations at the best vineyard in town. But
the Lord said, *Go this way*, so they did. Paul and his friends
remained flexible in their plans as they submitted to the leading of the Lord.

I don't like it when my plans change because of things outside my control. Maybe it's travel plans that get canceled or
an event that gets postponed because of bad weather. Even
more challenging is when it happens in marriage—when I think

we're doing one thing and Kristen is planning on something else. Sometimes we have separate ideas for how our evening or weekend will go and haven't had the chance to discuss our plans. Sometimes we're not even close to being aligned, and we realize we need to be flexible with our expectations and plans.

One of the core values of the church staff I help lead is that we want our team to "be flexible over frustrated." This means we value people who are willing to hold their plans loosely and not get frustrated when something unexpected happens. Most of our disappointments in life come from missed expectations. But if you're going to thrive in marriage and in parenting, you'll need to be ready for many unmet expectations.

Most of you reading this book have never been married. You're used to doing things your way, when you want it, and how you want it. But in marriage, God calls us to serve each other selflessly and sacrificially. You get the privilege of putting your spouse's needs before your own. For some of you who are laid back, this will come easy. For others who tend to be more set in your ways, you will be challenged to be flexible in marriage.[1]

And if God's future plan for you includes kids, they'll test your flexibility and expectations more than anything else in the world. Some of you are bringing kids into your new marriage from a prior relationship. You and your future spouse will need to be flexible in parenting, discipline, and expectations. It will serve you both well to hold on loosely to your plans and learn to communicate well with each other.

In what ways do you think you might struggle with being flexible in your new marriage? Discuss with your significant other how the two of you can choose to be flexible over frustrated.

God, we want to follow Your lead wherever You call us. If we want to go right but You want us to go left, then we'll want to go left. We desire to be flexible in following You wherever You call us. But also help us to be flexible spouses who adapt to each other's needs, wants, and desires. Help us to yield joyfully to the other and be flexible.

DAY 98

Joyful

You make known to me the path of life; you will fill me with
joy in your presence, with eternal pleasures at your right hand.

Psalm 16:11

I hope your wedding day will be one of the most joyful days
of your life. And I hope every day after brings you much joy
as well. The key to a joy-filled marriage isn't a great wedding
day but rather lives that are submitted to Christ. I encourage
all premarried couples to prepare for more than just their wedding day.

Just a few weeks ago, I watched two friends exchange wedding vows. I kept noticing how joyful they were to be together as
husband and wife. Their day had finally arrived, and it brought

them, their guests, and God loads of joy. But you need to know that no person on earth will ever bring you true joy. Your spouse will let you down, and your (future) kids will let you down. Your expectations won't always be met. But God will never let you down! He is the source of true joy, always.

In Psalm 16:11, David wrote, "You make known to me the path of life; you will fill me with joy in your presence, with eternal pleasures at your right hand." David knew the true source of joy isn't stuff, a great job, or even an incredible spouse and amazing kids. Joy is found in a relationship with the Father.

I confess there are moments when my life isn't marked with joy. God has given me an incredible spouse, four sons I love with everything in me, a job I'm passionate about, all the stuff I could ever want, and true friendships. If people and stuff could provide joy, then I should be the most joyful person on the planet. However, this isn't the case, because I often look for joy in all the wrong places. If you want to be a joyful spouse and marry a joyful spouse, then you need to look to the Father, for there is joy in His presence.

Don't you love seeing people whose lives are marked by joy? In a world so often marked by sadness and division, a person filled with joy lights up a room. What if your marriage and family were filled with this kind of joy? Think of the most joyful person you know. What can you learn from them about how to be more joyful in your relationship with your significant other and with your (future) kids?

> *God, we pray our marriage will be filled with joy. May our marriage and parenting be marked with joy because*

of Your love for us and because You are the source of joy. As life brings twists and turns and ups and downs, we pray our marriage won't be like the roller coaster of life but rather will be joyful because we know we can find all the joy we could ever want in You.

DAY 99

Helpful

So the man gave names to all the livestock, the birds in the sky and all the wild animals. But for Adam no suitable helper was found.

Genesis 2:20

In Genesis 1, the scene in the garden of Eden included a bunch of animals and one human being. Adam named the animals, enjoyed God's creativity in the uniqueness of each animal, and worked the garden. But he did not have a suitable helper to keep him company, to work the garden with him, or to be intimate with. God said it wasn't good for the man to be alone, so in Genesis 2:21–22, God created the woman, and the two soon became one flesh (v. 24).

One of the greatest benefits and joys of marriage is getting to walk through life with a companion. Among the many benefits of marriage, God provides you a helper in your spouse. I'm sure you've seen glimpses of this while dating and being engaged. Your significant other probably helps you in many ways. They can help with everyday tasks like shopping and moving furniture. They can help you make decisions when you're stuck. I love having a spouse who helps me decide between many good options. And your helper can help you grow spiritually. I love how Kristen spurs me on to become more like Jesus Christ (Heb. 10:24).

Perhaps nowhere in marriage is the need for a helper greater than in raising kids. When Kristen gave birth to our twins in 2004, we had no idea how hard the next minutes, hours, days, weeks, months, and years would be. We didn't know how challenging feeding, burping, and changing diapers would be. We had no clue how much a lack of sleep for weeks would affect us. And that was all easy compared to the emotional toil of raising teenagers. I'm so grateful God gave me a helper with whom to raise our sons (and I know Kristen would say the same about me).

God knew we would need help to get through life. And life with a helper is such a sweet gift the Lord gives us in marriage.

God, thank You that You always know exactly what we need in life. You knew it would not be good for us to be alone, so You provided us with the gifts of community and marriage. We pray that we would help each other become more like Your Son, Jesus. Thank You that You created us with a need for You and for others and that we can help each other in many ways.

DAY 100

Legacy-Minded

We will not hide them from their descendants; we will tell the next generation the praiseworthy deeds of the LORD, his power, and the wonders he has done.

Psalm 78:4

I didn't grow up in a Christian home. I thought I was a Christian simply because I wasn't Buddhist, Jewish, or Muslim. After I trusted in Christ as my Savior at age twenty-four, I wanted to change the trajectory of my family. While I love my family of origin, I began to pray I could leave behind a new and different legacy, one of godliness. I wanted there to be a fork in the road for my family and deeply hoped to change the legacy of the Kedersha name.

Thankfully, I believe Kristen and I will leave behind a godly legacy. All four of our sons love the Lord and are walking with

Jesus. They've placed their faith and trust in Jesus for the payment for and forgiveness of their sins. They've all been baptized and are serving at church. While we don't know what the future holds for them, we believe our children are headed in the right direction. And we pray they, in turn, will also leave behind a legacy of godliness.

You and your significant other are not married yet, but I challenge you to think of your legacy. One of the most important steps in determining your legacy is the decision you've recently made about whom you are going to marry. The only advice in the Bible about selecting a spouse is 2 Corinthians 6:14, when Paul said that believers should "not be yoked together with unbelievers." This means that a believer should not marry a nonbeliever. But the decision about whom to marry is much bigger than just whether your potential future spouse is a believer. You want to marry someone who loves Jesus as much as you do, with all their heart, soul, mind, and strength (Mark 12:30).

Choose to marry someone with whom you can leave behind a legacy of godliness that will carry forward for generation after generation. Tell the next generation the praiseworthy deeds of the Lord. Marry someone who will be on this mission with you. And pray you will leave behind a legacy of godliness.

Lord, we pray that we wouldn't just play the Christian game and halfheartedly pursue You. Rather, help us to love You with everything in us. Out of Your love for us and our love for You, help us do everything we can to leave behind a legacy of godliness. Help us to talk of Your deeds, power, and wonders to generation after generation.

Conclusion

Where Do We Go from Here?

Congratulations! You've made it to the end of this one-hundred-day prayer guide. You've now prayed together before getting married more than most married couples will do in their lifetime. If my prayers for you and this book have been answered, then you are now better prepared for marriage. Your significant other is now better prepared for marriage. And your marriage will now stand out as one that is built on the solid-rock foundation of Jesus Christ. I celebrate this with you!

I truly hope your prayer life as a couple is only just beginning. It's my prayer that you will continue this crucial habit every day together as husband and wife. It's my hope that you will continue to seek the Lord together and pray for each other and for your marriage. And I hope and pray you'll pursue the

Lord together in both the good moments and the not-so-good moments as husband and wife.

During your relationship, you will encounter some lows. Expectations will be missed, you'll likely hurt each other with your words and actions, and pride and selfishness will work against your one-flesh relationship. In those moments, you may be tempted to run away from each other and maybe even away from the Lord. But I want to remind you that there's nowhere better to turn than to the Lord. As Peter said to Jesus, "Lord, to whom shall we go? You have the words of eternal life. We have come to believe and to know that you are the Holy One of God" (John 6:68–69).

Where else will you turn in the highest highs and the lowest lows? It's my hope and prayer that you'll continue to pursue each other and daily seek the Lord together.

Ready or knot? Let's keep going.

Acknowledgments

Adam Tarnow: on March 31, 2022, I'd written only fifteen hundred words for this book. As I faced a looming writing deadline along with fears and insecurities, you challenged me to start writing every day. I took your challenge, and for the next one hundred days I wrote this book. Thank you for encouraging me and for celebrating the victories along the way.

To all the readers of *Ready or Knot?* and ScottKedersha .com, thanks for your support and ongoing encouragement. I'm deeply honored, and I pray anything I write or say helps you grow in your love for Jesus.

Nightlight Coffee & Donuts (Waco), Magnolia Press (Waco), and White Rhino Coffee (Waxahachie): not only do you serve some great coffee but you also provide the best coffee shop vibes for writing. I probably overstayed my welcome some days. Thank you for being my favorite places to write.

Baker Books team: thank you, once again, for giving me a shot to help couples. I'm grateful for a like-minded publisher who believes in me and in this message. Brian Vos, I'm honored to get to work with you again. You are best in class at what you do, and I'm thankful we got to partner together. Thank you for encouraging me to write. I hope this is just the beginning. I know there are many on the Baker team who helped bring this book to life—thank you! You shine in areas where I don't and I'm grateful for your gifts. Jennifer Stair, I'm so glad Baker brought you in again to help edit this book. You made it so much better! You're a great editor, but more than anything you affirm and encourage me.

Harris Creek Baptist Church: thank you for being my family's home church and for helping me become more like Jesus Christ. I've gotten a second chance in ministry after almost burning out. Thank you to the staff and elders for supporting and affirming me in my role and in my writing. Specific thanks to the E Team and Family Team. I hope we run together a long time. I love you, friends. And a very special shoutout to my *More Than Roommates* teammates, Derek Davidson and Gabrielle McCullough. You are a blast and such a joy to work with.

JP, I'm so grateful to you for writing the foreword to this book. Thank you for your support and care. Thank you for taking the time to develop me and help me grow. Thanks for being my pastor and for spurring me on to become more like Jesus. Clofficemates for life!

My community: thanks to my many friends for your support. At the risk of forgetting some people, there are a few I want to thank by name. To our life group at Harris Creek (Eckerts, Ivys, Shearers, and Walkers), thanks for being such great friends and for your encouragement. Our lives are better because you're in them. Thanks to all my friends who let me tell their stories in this book. Byron Weathersbee, thank you for being a thought partner from day one with this book. You helped me see the value in it before I even wrote one word. Wes Butler—thanks for listening, encouraging, challenging, and supporting me in every part of my walk with Jesus. I don't know what I'd do without our friendship. To all my friends in Dallas and at Watermark, I miss and love you! Thank you to my family and Kristen's family for being so loving and supportive of us and our sons.

Duncan, Drew, Carson, and Lincoln: I'm grateful our love continues to grow over the years. I never knew how much I would love being a dad, and I'm so proud of you and the young men you're becoming. Your mom and I are grateful we're leaving behind a legacy of godliness with the four of you.

Kristen: all my words fall short. Thank you for carrying the rock on mornings, evenings, and weekends when I needed to write. Thanks for editing, praying, and brainstorming with me on this book. You are the second greatest example of the Lord's kindness in my life and my second greatest love. I'm thankful this needs no explanation to you.

Most of all, thank You, Lord. I hope I never, ever get over my salvation. Thank You that You are the perfection of every attribute described in this book. "However, I consider my life worth nothing to me; my only aim is to finish the race and complete the task the Lord Jesus has given me—the task of testifying to the good news of God's grace" (Acts 20:24).

Notes

Introduction What I Wish I Knew before I Said "I Do"

1. Lavern Nissley, "An Amazing Secret to Marriage Success," Encompass Connection Center, March 26, 2019, https://www.encompasscc.org/blog/an-amazing-secret-to-marriage-success. See also Christopher G. Ellison, Amy M. Burdette, and W. Bradford Wilcox, "The Couple That Prays Together: Race and Ethnicity, Religion, and Relationship Quality Among Working-Age Adults," *Journal of Marriage and Family* 72, no. 4 (August 2010): 963–75, https://www.jstor.org/stable/40864957.

2. Scott Kedersha, *Ready or Knot? 12 Conversations Every Couple Needs to Have before Marriage* (Grand Rapids: Baker Books, 2019).

3. If you're curious, my response to my friend included eight attributes (humble, initiating, servant-minded, loving, selfless, steadfast, abiding, and joyful). This initial draft years ago formed the basis for this very book you're reading.

Day 5 Holy

1. Gary Thomas, *Sacred Marriage: What If God Designed Marriage to Make Us Holy More Than to Make Us Happy?* (Grand Rapids: Zondervan, 2015), 11.

2. Kedersha, *Ready or Knot?*, 82.

Day 10 Committed

1. While commitment is a key trait in a husband and wife, I always counsel a victim of abuse to seek immediate safety, wisdom, and help. In cases of abuse, please reach out to a trusted friend, pastor, or counselor.

Day 12 Kingdom-Minded

1. Gary Thomas, *A Lifelong Love: Discovering How Intimacy with God Breathes Passion into Your Marriage* (Colorado Springs: David C. Cook, 2015), 41.

Day 22 Disciplined

1. Adam Grant (@AdamMGrant), "To understand success, pay less attention to the final product and more to the mundane process," Twitter post, May 28, 2018, 9:03 a.m., https://twitter.com/adammgrant/status/10011015 80417019904?lang=en.

Day 28 Prayerful

1. Jackie Hill Perry (@jackiehillperry), Instagram post, May 24, 2022, https://www.instagram.com/p/Cd8CH5OuznN.

Day 34 Thoughtful

1. The Enneagram is a helpful tool that can help you grow your marriage. If you have questions about the Enneagram, check out some of the resources from Beth and Jeff McCord at becomingus.com.

Day 35 Celebratory

1. Dr. Gary Chapman, *The 5 Love Languages: The Secret to a Love That Lasts* (1992; repr., Chicago: Northfield, 2015). For more on these five love languages, see 5lovelanguages.com.

Day 40 Obedient

1. What does it look like to be obedient to God with our money? A full understanding is beyond the scope of this book, but I'd start by reading Matthew 6:19–24, where Jesus tells us we can't serve both God and money. Check out chapter 5 of *Ready or Knot?* for a better understanding of marriage and money. If you want a thorough resource about money, I recommend Randy Alcorn's *Money, Possessions, and Eternity: A Comprehensive Guide to What the Bible Says about Financial Stewardship, Generosity, Materialism, Retirement, Financial Planning, Gambling, Debt, and More* (Carol Stream, IL: Tyndale, 2021).

Day 46 Respectful

1. Thomas L. Constable, "Notes on Ephesians, 2022 Edition," Constable's Expository (Bible Study) Notes, accessed January 18, 2023, https://www.plano biblechapel.org/tcon/notes/html/nt/ephesians/ephesians.htm#head45.

2. Chapman, *5 Love Languages*.

3. You can take a free quiz to learn your love language at 5lovelanguages .com/quizzes/love-language/.

Day 51 Dependable

1. It's often stated that Christians and non-Christians have the same divorce rate. This is not accurate. The divorce rate for faithful, committed followers of Christ is significantly lower than the divorce rate of non-Christians or casual Christians. See "Is the Divorce Rate among Christians Truly the Same as among non-Christians?," Got Questions, updated January 4, 2022, https://www.got questions.org/Christian-divorce-rate.html.

Day 55 Merciful

1. In cases of ongoing addiction, part of showing mercy is finding help for your spouse with a pastor, counselor, or recovery ministry. In cases of abuse, make sure you're safe and work with others to get the help your spouse needs. That might include a pastor, counselor, or even law enforcement.

Day 58 Trustworthy

1. Kristen is five feet, eleven inches tall and has brown hair and blue eyes with streaks of yellow. This means my standard of beauty is five feet, eleven inches tall, brown hair, and blue eyes with streaks of yellow. While you can find people other than your spouse to be attractive, your spouse should be your standard and definition of beauty for the rest of your lives.

Day 61 Pure

1. I write about more specific ways to fight for purity in chapter 8 of *Ready or Knot?*. I also encourage you to read some of my blog posts on purity by searching for "purity" or "pornography" at scottkedersha.com/search.

Day 66 Loving

1. If you'd like more details on this exercise, check out my post "A Practical Way to Encourage Your Spouse," *Scott Kedersha* (blog), September 12, 2021, https:// www.scottkedersha.com/blog-pages/a-practical-way-to-encourage-your-spouse.

Day 70 Curious

1. Both are married, just not to each other.

Day 78 Playful

1. This is why I started the *More Than Roommates* podcast with my friends Derek and Gabrielle. We want to help couples take the next step to be more intentional in their marriage so that they can be so much more than just roommates.

2. If you need a refresher on the importance of fun, friendship, and playfulness in marriage, see chapter 10 of *Ready or Knot?*.

Day 80 Healthy

1. For some people, being overweight is not due to unhealthy eating or exercise habits. Ongoing health issues and genetics affect many people in ways that are outside their control. I share this example from my life because it's been an area where I've depended on my wife to help me make healthy decisions about eating, exercise, and sleep.

Day 81 Cherishing

1. Gary Thomas, *Cherish: The One Word That Changes Everything for Your Marriage* (Grand Rapids: Zondervan, 2017), 15.

2. Thomas, *Cherish*, 18, emphasis in original.

Day 87 Persevering

1. Angela Duckworth, *Grit: The Power of Passion and Perseverance* (New York: Scribner, 2018).

2. Pine Cove, "True Love and True Grit," *The Pine Cove Podcast* season 3, episode 6 (April 28, 2022), https://www.pinecove.com/blog/podcast-3-6/.

Day 88 Marked by Integrity

1. Unless, of course, you have a child attending each school, meaning your tuition money gives you permission to cheer for as many teams as you'd like.

2. Merriam-Webster, s.v. "integrity," accessed January 18, 2023, https://www.merriam-webster.com/dictionary/integrity.

3. The best choice here is not to cuss at all. As Paul said in Ephesians 4:29, "Do not let any unwholesome talk come out of your mouths."

Day 95 Selfless

1. I describe this story in more detail in chapter 2 of *Ready or Knot?*.

Day 97 Flexible

1. Some of you were hoping being "flexible" referred to bedroom activities. That's a subject for another book, but you're free to pray for that as well.

About the Author

Scott Kedersha is the marriage pastor at Harris Creek Baptist Church. Over the last seventeen years as a marriage pastor, he has helped more than five thousand couples answer the question, "Ready or Knot?" He is the author of the book *Ready or Knot?*, the cohost of the *More Than Roommates* podcast, and lives in Waco, Texas, with his wife and four sons. Learn more at www.ScottKedersha.com.

Connect with Scott:

@SKedersha

@SKedersha & @MoreThanRoommates

@SKedersha

Get Intentional about Your Marriage

LISTEN TO SCOTT'S PODCAST

Welcome to *More Than Roommates*, where we want to help you take the next step to be more intentional in your marriage. We hope that through authentic, biblical, and practical conversation you will gain tools and wisdom to help you take one step closer to the Lord and the marriage He intends for you and your spouse. Listen in as Scott Kedersha, Gabrielle McCullough, and Derek Davidson help you intentionally strengthen your relationship.

Listen wherever podcasts are found

Connect with Scott, Gabrielle, and Derek
on Instagram **@MoreThanRoommates**